A SHORT HISTORY
OF THE CORPS OF
ROYAL ENGINEERS

D1335552

The Cap Badge
in full-colour for use on
sign-boards etc

The Cap Badge worn
by officers and soldiers in
Nos 1 and 2 Dress and
by soldiers on berets

The Corps Badge (The Royal Arms)
granted by King William IV in 1832

THE BADGES
OF THE CORPS

The Corps Cipher for use
on letterheads and the
banners of the Fanfare
Trumpets of the RE Band

The Corps Colours as used on
unit flags and plaques and the
Tactical Recognition Flash

GRENADE BADGES

Officer's Beret
Badge

Arm Badge worn
above the chevrons
by SSgts and Sgts

Soldiers' Collar Badge
No 2 Dress

Officers' Collar
Badge No 2 Dress

A SHORT HISTORY OF THE CORPS OF ROYAL ENGINEERS

I have stated it plain, an' my argument's thus
("It's all one," says the Sapper)
There's only one Corps which is perfect – that's us;
An' they call us Her Majesty's Engineers,
Her Majesty's Royal Engineers,
With the rank and pay of a Sapper!

— Rudyard Kipling

The Institution of Royal Engineers
CHATHAM
2006

First published 2006 by
The Institution of Royal Engineers,
Brompton Barracks, Chatham, Kent ME4 4UG, UK.

British Library Cataloguing in Publication Data:
a catalogue record for this book is available from the British Library

ISBN (10): 0-903530-28-7
ISBN (13): 978-0903530-28-6

Compiled by Lieutenant Colonel M. D. Cooper, MBE, with assistance from
Colonel G. W. A. Napier, the Corps Historian, and Lieutenant Colonel R. A. Dudin, MBE,
(author of *The Royal Engineers on Operation Telic*)
Editor-in-Chief Lieutenant Colonel D. N. Hamilton, MBE
Editing and Picture Research by Captain J. E. Borer

Designed and edited by David Gibbons,
DAG Publications Ltd, London.
Production by Hugh Allan.

Printed in China by Compass Press

Publisher's Note: The first edition was compiled at Headquarters 11 Engineer Group, Minley,
in 1991 by Major D. P. Aston, assisted by Mrs Susan Presland, Mrs Mary Boyle and Mrs Claire
Cunningham. This second edition is a revision of the work carried out by Major Aston and his
team and also incorporates additional material from 1991 to 2005, using the sources
mentioned on page 6.

Every effort has been made to ensure the accuracy of the information presented in this
book, but there will inevitably be the occasional conflict of data when comparing sources.
The publisher welcomes comments and corrections from readers, all of which will be
considered for future editions.

Acknowledgements: All illustrations are copyright The Institution of Royal Engineers except
the following for which we are grateful for reproduction permission being granted. The Royal
Military Canal is reproduced by courtesy of the Railway and Canal Historical Society. The map
showing the states of the Former Yugoslavia was drawn by Mrs Jacqui Thorndick of the
Institution of Royal Engineers.

CONTENTS

Preface, 6
Introduction, 7
Bishop Gundulph, 8
Early Days, 9
The Invention of Gunpowder and the Development of Cannon, 9
The Civil War and Formation of the Standing Army, 10
The War of the Spanish Succession, 11
The Beginnings of the Corps of Engineers, 11
The First Engineer Soldiers, 12
Onwards and Expansion, 14
Sieges, Saps and Sappers, 15
The Napoleonic Wars, Expansion and a Third Corps, 16
Retrenchment and Peace, 20
The Crimean War, 22
Years of Development and Small Wars, 24
War in South Africa, a Cap Badge and a Song, 30
Modernization, 32
The Great War, 35
A Troubled Peace, 39
The Second World War, 43
Post-war Winds of Change, 55
The End of National Service and More Small Wars, 64
Northern Ireland, 69
Changes Continue but Variety Remains, 74
The South Atlantic, 78
Major Changes and the End of the Cold War, 80
Options for Change and the Strategic Defence Review, 82
War in the Middle East, 87
The Balkans, 88
Toys for the Boys, 100
Into the Millennium, 103
The Iraq War, 112
Organization of the Corps, 118
Esprit de Corps, 124
New Beginnings: An Army for the Future, 126
Annex 1. The Victoria Crosses of the Corps, 129
Annex 2. The George Crosses of the Corps, 131
Annex 3. The Corps March, 131
Annex 4. The Corps Song, 132

PREFACE

The history of the Royal Engineers is inextricably tied up with the history of military engineering, so, although the several forbears of the present Corps date from various years in the eighteenth century, our history really starts in 1066 when William, Duke of Normandy, arrived from France and defeated King Harold at Hastings. It could thus be said that there can be no such thing as a 'short history'!

The written history is tied up in several publications, the main ones being the eleven, and soon to be twelve, volumes of the official *History of the Corps of Royal Engineers*, articles in *The Royal Engineers Journal* and *The Sapper* magazine, *The Royal Engineers on Operation Telic* and other publications, notably the books *Royal Engineers* by Derek Boyd, and

Follow The Sapper and *The Sapper VCs* by Colonel Gerald Napier. The raison d'être for a 'short' history is thus to bring all these things together in a condensed form and hopefully inspire the reader to delve further into all the other publications.

Having said that, although this edition will be on sale through RE Corps Enterprises and the RE Museum Shop, its primary function is to inform, and hopefully instil a sense of pride and belonging to, new members of our Corps. It will thus be a free issue to all RE soldier recruits at the Army Training Regiment, Lichfield, and RE officer cadets at the Royal Military Academy, Sandhurst.

Lieutenant Colonel D. N. Hamilton, MBE
Secretary, The Institution of Royal Engineers

Mounted Sappers blowing up a bridge in South Africa during the Boer War. From a series of sketches by Lance Corporal Everard.

INTRODUCTION

From the earliest times, man's ingenuity has made use of defences to protect him from his enemies. In addition to utilizing natural defences and obstacles, man also began to develop his own defences. This required practitioners of education and skill, not only to design and build them, but also to select the most advantageous locations for them.

> *"To secure peace is to prepare for war"*
> – General Carl Von Clausewitz

The ancient Greeks, Romans and Chinese all had access to such knowledge and ability. In Britain, the Roman influence still endures, from their invasion and subsequent occupation of England, when their military engineers set up a network of fortifications and military roads. Towns whose names end in 'chester' or 'caster' are sites of Roman camps – for example, Chichester, Colchester and Doncaster. Roads such as 'Watling Street', from Dover to Wroxeter via Chatham and London, and 'The Fosseway', from Lincoln to Exeter, which were part of the Roman network of military roads, survive to this day. Hadrian's Wall, from Newcastle to Carlisle, is a well-known surviving Roman border defence, while Offa's Dyke, an earthwork stretching from Chester to Chepstow, is an example of home-grown Saxon field engineering. Indeed, the word 'engineer' is derived from the Latin, *ingenarius*, which originally meant a person skilled in the art of constructing defences for the protection of settlements or towns. The word was later applied to those who constructed works of public utility.

The Military Engineer was thus the precursor of the Civil Engineer. Throughout the history of the British army, its Military Engineers have never been short of men skilled both in the profession of arms and in the fields of military and civil engineering.

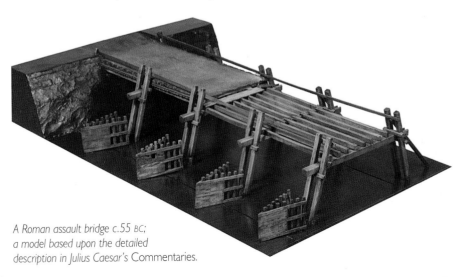

A Roman assault bridge c.55 BC; a model based upon the detailed description in Julius Caesar's Commentaries.

BISHOP GUNDULPH

Historically, the Corps of Royal Engineers can claim direct descent from the Military Engineers brought to this country from Normandy in 1066 by William the Conqueror. Chief of these was a Norman knight called Humphrey de Tilleul, who is depicted in the Bayeux Tapestry supervising the construction of a fort, or *castellum*. These were transported by sea from Normandy in prefabricated sections and erected on an earth mound formed by the soil excavated from a circular moat surrounding it, an early example of the Operation 'Overlord' Mulberry Harbour technique in 1944 and also of what we now understand as force protection.

After his victory at the Battle of Hastings, William exploited to the north-west, leaving Humphrey to safeguard the Hastings beachhead. Regrettably, Humphrey defected back to Normandy when he received rumours of his wife's infidelity, and William's army commander, Eustache Fiennes, was obliged to appoint a man in his place. This was a young monk called Gundulph – with no family problems.

In those days the Church was the seat of learning and education, where capable men could be found, and there was nothing strange in appointing a monk to be the King's principal Military Engineer. Indeed, it could be said that in engineering terms there

"We will either find a way or make one." – Hannibal

was little difference between designing and building a great abbey and a great fortress. Gundulph was skilled in the art of siege warfare, being able to construct and operate the crude engines of war necessary to break a fortress wall, or to tunnel beneath it. His first construction task was to build a great edifice to overawe the Saxon citizens of London. This mighty structure still stands today as the White Tower in the Tower of London. He also strengthened the castle at Rochester. Promoted in the Church, Gundulph became Bishop of Rochester and enlarged his cathedral, where his tower, Gundulph's Tower, still stands at the cathedral entrance, another monument to his skill. Today it is appropriate that in the seat of the Corps' founding father repose many Royal Engineer memorials and that each year it hosts the Corps Memorial Service.

Statue of Bishop Gundulph at Rochester Cathedral.

Gundulph achieved a rare duality: eminence both as a churchman and as a military engineer. He is thus an example to all in the Corps who strive to be both good professional soldiers and good professional engineers, and it is he, rather than Humphrey de Tilleul, who is held to be the founding father of the Corps.

EARLY DAYS

In the early days there was no standing army. Troops were raised as required for particular campaigns and returned to their normal lives afterwards. Engineers were similarly employed, but usually for only as long as their services were required, although it is known that the King permanently employed a few, Waldivius Ingeniator being one mentioned in the Domesday Book of 1086.

The Military Engineers of King Richard I, who reigned from 1189 to 1199, were among the finest castle-builders in the world, and during the Crusades they proved that they were equally skilled in assaulting fortified places in the Holy Land. King Edward I (1272–1307), in his campaigns against the Welsh and Scots, employed vast numbers of men to build military roads leading into mountain strongholds, and to build castles, some of which still stand today. It was during these campaigns that an assault floating bridge was constructed across the Menai Straits. Meanwhile, throughout the Middle Ages the threat of invasion from the French, Spanish and, later, the Dutch required the construction of seaward defences and fortifications in the Thames estuary, the Medway and other naval ports.

THE INVENTION OF GUNPOWDER AND THE DEVELOPMENT OF CANNON

English military engineers were first employed overseas at the siege of Calais and the Battle of Crécy in 1346. They included miners impressed from the Forest of Dean and smiths and other artificers from the City of London. Cannon were used by the English for the first time in this campaign. The gun was originally a static weapon and highly dangerous to fire. As it developed it slowly superseded the great, cumbersome engines of war, and this in turn brought about a complete reappraisal of the design of fortifications, as well as a more sophisticated approach to the science of siege warfare. With these developments it became necessary to establish an organization to administer the King's cannon, his arsenals, castles and other fortifications, as well as to supervise a growing armaments industry springing up in London. This organization was set up in Gundulph's White Tower and was called

The Arms of the Board of Ordnance, 1806.

The Office of Ordnance. (This was because a cannon was referred to as a piece of ordnance, as it still is to this day.)

Nicholas Merbury, who had been Henry V's Chief Engineer at Harfleur and at Agincourt in 1415, was made the first Master of the King's Works and Ordnance, and his Office of Ordnance was established for engineer and gunner officers. In time of war it raised Ordnance Trains of gunners, engineers and storemen suitable for the campaigns and siege operations on which it was intended to embark. At the conclusion of hostilities, such Trains were disbanded.

The Office of Ordnance was renamed the Board of Ordnance in 1518 during the reign of Henry VIII (1509–47). The gunners and engineers held on its permanent establishment, with others temporarily enrolled in time of war to form Trains, were in effect a private army of the Board of Ordnance. The board regulated their terms of service, their promotion and salaries, exercising strict control over them in peace and even on active service.

THE CIVIL WAR AND FORMATION OF THE STANDING ARMY

The Civil Wars lasted from 1642 to 1651, during which Oliver Cromwell raised the New Model Army, which as a force was very efficient for its day. Its General of Horse and later its Lord General (in our terms Commander-in-Chief) was Sir Thomas Fairfax. Its Train included a Chief Engineer and a Master Gunner, six Assistant Engineers, three Captains and three Lieutenants of Pioneers, and a Battery Master. The Engineers of Cromwell's Army carried out some remarkable river-crossing operations.

"A few honest men are better than numbers."
– Oliver Cromwell, Lord Protector of England

The restoration of the monarchy and the return of King Charles II in 1660 brought about the formation of a permanent standing army of cavalry and infantry. At the same time, the gunner and engineer establishment of the Board of Ordnance was revised, but the staff of the Military Branch of the Ordnance remained a separate body.

In order to improve their professionalism, young engineer officers were sent by the board to Europe to study the science of fortification and siege warfare, there being no academy or college in England where such subjects were taught. From Tudor days the country had relied very much upon its island geography for defence, and it was the traditional task of the Navy to keep an invading army from landing.

The Portuguese-born wife of King Charles II, Catherine of Braganza, brought with her as dowry the cities of Tangier and Calcutta, to which British troops had to be deployed for their protection. These were the forerunners of the many overseas garrisons of the future British Empire in which engineer units served. The reign of King Charles II also saw the formation of the Honourable East India Company, which later raised the three famous Indian engineer Corps of Madras, Bengal and Bombay Sappers and Miners. These eventually became part of the Royal Indian Engineers and then, in 1947, part of the Indian Army.

THE WAR OF THE SPANISH SUCCESSION

In 1688 Charles II's successor, James II, was deposed, allowing William of Orange to reign jointly with his consort Mary until 1702. He subjugated Ireland, which had espoused the cause of the deposed king and in 1692 undertook major military operations on the continent of Europe. These ended in 1697, but hostilities broke out again in 1701 when the so-called War of the Spanish Succession started. This war lasted 12 years and involved operations in Spain, Gibraltar, Portugal, Minorca, North America and at sea. Engineers were employed in all the land campaigns, and many served afloat with the Fleet. The Duke of Marlborough fought nine campaigns in the Low Countries, supported by siege trains of an unprecedented size. As an example, the train used in 1708 at the capture of the powerful fortress of Lille consisted of vast quantities of engineer siege equipment, 100 guns, 60 mortars of varying calibres up to fifteen inches, over 3,000 wagons and 15,000 horses – the whole taking up a road space of 24 kilometres.

> *"There is one certain means by which I can be sure to never see my country's ruin: I will die in the last ditch"* – William III (William of Orange), King of England

THE BEGINNINGS OF THE CORPS OF ENGINEERS

The War of the Spanish Succession ended with the Treaty of Utrecht. This brought about the disbandment of the greater part of the army and all the trains. Only a small number of officers were retained on the Board of Ordnance permanent establishment; but of these the Gunners were disgruntled at their subordinate position to the Engineers; and the Engineers were displeased at the lower

Brigadier Michael Richards, Chief Engineer of England 1711–1714.

salary authorized. Brigadier General Michael Richards, the Chief Engineer, proposed a scheme for increasing the efficiency and size of the establishment by disposing of outdated appointments. In parallel, he strongly supported a recommendation for a regimental establishment of the Artillery whereby the 'Stores of Artillery and Fortifications might be cheaper and better looked after'. Initially, the recommendations were not accepted by the Board. But when it was found that no serviceable cannon could be produced to oppose the Jacobite Rising of 1715, Richards's arguments were driven home. On 26 May 1716, by Warrant of King George I, the Artillery was placed on a separate establishment, and the Royal Regiment of Artillery was born. At the same time, the

Corps of Engineers was born, consisting of 28 engineers who were all officers – rank and file continued to be raised as required for each campaign. It is interesting to note, however, that for the next hundred and fifty years engineer officers remained responsible for the siting and construction of batteries in siege operations from which the artillery fired their guns.

Although the artillery and engineers were now part of the regular forces, they were still in effect the 'private army' of the Board of Ordnance and were not directly controlled by the commander-in-chief of the army as were the cavalry and infantry. In 1741 the board established the Royal Military Academy at Woolwich for 'instructing the people of its Military branch to form good Officers of Artillery and perfect Engineers', but it was not until 1799 that the Royal Military College was formed at Sandhurst to train officers for the cavalry and infantry.

THE FIRST ENGINEER SOLDIERS

There were now permanent military engineer officers, but the tradesmen and labourers required for engineer work in peace had to be found from locally employed civilians. For active service, tradesmen were temporarily enlisted for the Ordnance Trains, or working parties were found from the infantry. This system was often found to be less than satisfactory.

Gibraltar had been captured from the Spanish in 1704, and it was important to improve its fortifications because of the continuing threat from Spain. Civilian tradesmen carried out this work, super-vised by engineer officers. However, the tradesmen often proved unreliable, and infantrymen could not be spared from the garrison. Lieutenant Colonel William Green, the Commanding Engineer at Gibraltar, therefore suggested to the Governor, General Eliott (who himself had been an Engineer officer in his earlier days) that a unit be raised under military discipline to supply a constant and trustworthy supply of skilled labour. This unit would also provide a valuable addition to the military strength of the fortress. This was agreed, and, under a Royal Warrant dated 6 March 1772, a Company of Soldier Artificers was raised by transfers of suitable men from the regiments in the garrison.

The Royal Warrant authorized the company strength as follows:

1 Sergeant-Major with pay at 3s 0d per day (15p)
3 Sergeants with pay at 1s 6d per day (7.5p)
3 Corporals with pay at 1s 2d per day (about 6p)
60 Privates with pay at 10d per day (about 4p)
1 Drummer with pay at 10d per day (about 4p)

The privates' trades were to be stonecutters, masons, miners, lime-burners, carpenters, smiths, gardeners or wheelwrights, and the company was to be commanded by officers of the Corps of Engineers. Sergeant Major Ince became well known for the work of his company, and his name lives on in Gibraltar today. Indeed, it was his idea to cut a tunnel in which guns could be sited into the north face of The Rock.

This first company of regular engineer soldiers was gradually increased in strength and, during the Great Siege of Gibraltar from 1779 to 1783, proved its effectiveness. The many defences and batteries built by these men and the famous galleries hewn by them in the north face remain, to this day, as a memorial to their work. In 1786, with a now well-established reputation, the company's strength was raised to 275 and then subsequently divided into two companies. Boy Artificers were also enlisted, and they may be regarded as the forerunners of the modern Military Apprentice. (An accurate model of Gibraltar made by Boy Artificers can be seen in the Royal Engineers Museum at Chatham.)

Soldier Artificers in their 1786 red uniforms.

ONWARDS AND EXPANSION

In May 1757 the officers of the Corps of Engineers were given military rank for the first time:

Chief Engineer became Major General
Director became Lieutenant Colonel
Sub-director became Major
Engineer-in-Ordinary became Captain
Engineer Extraordinary became Captain Lieutenant
Sub-engineer became Lieutenant
Practitioner became Ensign or Second Lieutenant

Thirty years later a Royal Warrant dated 25 April 1787 granted the officers the 'royal' title so that they now became the Corps of Royal Engineers.

The threat of invasion after the French Revolution showed how vulnerable our coastline was. In 1786, the Duke of Richmond, then Master General of the Ordnance, had difficulty in obtaining government funds for his schemes to fortify the Portsmouth and Plymouth dockyards. He therefore proposed that a corps of military artificers be formed, like that already established in Gibraltar, thereby effecting considerable economy in executing the works. His proposal was accepted, and on 10 October 1787 a Corps of Royal Military Artificers was raised, the Military Artificers to be officered, as before, by the Corps of Royal Engineers. Six companies were authorized, each of 100 men established as:

> "All might be free if they valued freedom, and defended it as they should."
> – Samuel Adams, Father of the American Revolution

1 Sergeant Major with pay at 2s 3d per day (11p)
3 Sergeants with pay at 1s 9d per day (9p)
4 Corporals with pay at 1s 7d per day (8p)
12 Carpenters)
10 Masons)
10 Bricklayers)
5 Smiths)
5 Wheelwrights)
4 Sawyers) with pay at 9d per day (4p)
8 Miners)
2 Painters)
2 Coopers)
2 Collar makers)
30 Labourers with pay at 6d per day (2½p)
2 Drummers with pay at 9d per day (4p)

Working pay, not exceeding 9d (4p) per day, was also to be given for the days that were actually employed on works.

Royal Military Artificers in their Board of Ordnance blue uniforms of 1792.

The companies were not mobile and were stationed at Woolwich, Chatham, Portsmouth, Gosport, Plymouth and on the Channel Islands, one company being split between Jersey and Guernsey. Two additional companies were authorized in 1793 for overseas service, and in June 1797 the two original Gibraltar companies were incorporated into the Royal Military Artificers. At this point they lost their scarlet coats, worn since their formation, because the Artificers were to be dressed in blue.

Further reorganization was authorized by a Warrant dated 5 September 1806. Two additional companies were raised, and for the first time numbers identified them. They were now stationed as follows:

1st Company	Woolwich
2nd Company	Chatham
3rd Company	Dover
4th Company	Portsmouth
5th Company	Gosport
6th Company	Plymouth
7th Company	Spike Island, Southern Ireland
8th Company	Channel Islands
9th and 10th Companies	Gibraltar
11th Company	West Indies
12th Company	Nova Scotia

The strength per company was subsequently raised from 100 to 126. It is from this era that the present-day size and composition of the basic engineer unit has developed. However, the fact that the companies were static proved detrimental. Despite the increases in the number and size of companies, detachments still had to be found for overseas campaigns, and commanders naturally retained their best men rather than sending them to the field army.

SIEGES, SAPS AND SAPPERS

One of the main military tasks of Engineers in most field armies of the 17th, 18th and 19th centuries was the practice of siege warfare against fortresses. If the defenders could not be starved into submission, the walls had to be breached. Infantry would then assault through the breach to capture the fortress. This could be done by either mining underneath the walls and exploding a large gunpowder charge or by battering them down with artillery fire. Engineers were engaged in both processes. To get near enough to the defences but still retain some protection, trenches were dug towards the fortress.

The system of trenches could be quite complicated in layout, and they could not be dug in the normal way by men digging downwards from ground level because the men would be exposed to fire from the defenders. Trenches were therefore dug in a zig-zag pattern and at progressively deeper levels towards the enemy – the process being known as sapping.

Each sapper, that is the builder of a sap, carried a pick and shovel and two empty gabions, which were rather like wicker baskets that could be placed on the exposed

"The general prizes most the fortress which took the longest siege."
– Edward Garrett

flank and filled with excavated soil to give cover from enemy fire. The leading sapper could therefore work in a relatively shallow trench yet still have sufficient cover from the flank. To give him cover at the exposed end of the trench he used a stuffed gabion or sap roller, which he pushed forward as the work advanced. The stuffed gabion was of larger diameter than a normal gabion and was filled with faggots or brushwood. In the rear of the first sapper, a second sapper dug the trench deeper, and behind him third, fourth and fifth men each worked at progressively lower levels to deepen the trench. Tightly lashed bundles of sticks called fascines were also placed on top of the gabions on the flank to raise the height of the cover. The sapper also prepared emplacements for the attacking guns as the trench digging advanced.

THE NAPOLEONIC WARS, EXPANSION AND A THIRD CORPS

The 19th century opened with the beginning of a decade-and-a-half struggle between Great Britain and Napoleon Bonaparte, First Consul, then Emperor of France. In 1808 Napoleon intended to subdue Spain and place his brother Joseph on the throne in Madrid. As Great Britain had a treaty with Portugal, an army was sent to protect Lisbon and to form a base from which Napoleon's forces could be driven back to France. So started the Peninsular War, which was to have a far-reaching influence on the British army, and its Engineers in particular. Initially, the British army under Sir John Moore was outnumbered and obliged to withdraw after fighting a rearguard action at Corunna. Another expedition was planned immediately, and more troops and supplies were landed at Lisbon in 1809 under the command of Arthur Wellesley (later Duke of Wellington).

> "We have had such an expenditure of Engineers that I can hardly wish for anybody, lest the same fate befall him as has befallen so many." – Wellington

To defend the base at Lisbon, three lines of defence works, called the Lines of Torres Vedras, were dug. Wellesley started the campaign with only 11 Royal Engineer officers and 28 Royal Military Artificers. Only 18 artificers were employed on the lines with up to 7,000 Portuguese labourers conscripted to carry out the works. A single artificer was therefore required to supervise some 500–700 labourers!

In addition to being responsible for siting, preparing and repairing gun platforms during sieges, Royal Engineer officers also led infantry assaulting parties carrying scaling ladders to place against walls and fascines to throw into ditches. In this duty they invariably suffered heavy casualties: during the Peninsular War, 23 out of 103 Royal Engineer officers engaged were killed in action. But their offensive combat engineering skills did not match their abilities and experience in fortification. There was no suggestion that they lacked courage or resourcefulness in all these duties, but it became apparent that the French Engineers were much better trained and equipped than their British counterparts. In a report to London, a somewhat frustrated and critical Wellington wrote: 'These great losses could be avoided and, in my opinion, time gained in every siege, if we had properly trained people to carry them on. It is a cruel situation to be placed in, and I earnestly request your Lordship to have a Corps of Sappers and Miners formed without loss of time.'

In fact, the static nature of the engineer arm had been recognized before this. In 1799, the Duke of York, Commander-in-Chief of the Army, had planned an expedition to northern Holland, but the Board of Ordnance could not provide any engineers. The Duke, therefore, raised his own Engineers by taking volunteers who had been tradesmen from infantry regiments. The function of this unit, the Royal Staff Corps, was 'to construct Field Works and to do other Military Duties of whatsoever nature, in the Quartermaster General's Department'. At the end of 1808, the Commander-in-Chief sent out a circular letter explaining: 'The principal purpose for which this Corps was established was to enable the Quartermaster General to give the most effectual assistance towards the Construction of Field Works, Bridges, Roads, and the superintendence of all labour comprised under the term Field Engineering. And every possible care has been taken to introduce proper and capable persons into this Corps, both officers and men, for the performance of these duties.'

The Royal Staff Corps Companies were not more than 50 Artificers strong, but it could be said they were the direct ancestors of the Royal Engineer Field Companies. During the Peninsular War they carried out some really valuable construction work and field engineering, while a

The Lines of Torres Vedras.

lasting monument to their work in England is the Royal Military Canal that runs westwards from Shorncliffe to Rye.

Captain (later General) Charles William Pasley, RE, was no less a critic of the Royal Military Artificers – and, indeed, of the Royal Engineers! An experienced campaigner, he had been airing his views for some time on the capabilities in the field of both Corps. Of the Royal Military Artificers, he wrote: 'All the companies were kept permanently fixed at their respective stations both at home and abroad, where they remained for life, in a state of vegetation, so that there were at that period a vast number of men who had actually grown grey in the Corps who had never entered a transport nor made a single day's march from the headquarters of their Company. Everywhere they intermixed with civilians, they married in a proportion unknown in any other Corps, so much so that the number of women and children belonging to one company was often equal to that of a battalion of the line.'

Pasley had been on Sir John Moore's staff until after the Battle of Corunna. Following wounds in a later engagement, he took command of the Artificer Company at Plymouth. There he began a system of instruction in fieldworks that was to transform the Corps. Other events occurred that added to this transformation. A Royal Warrant dated 28 May 1811 almost doubled the strength of the Royal Military Artificers, and at the same time the companies were no longer localized but rotated between stations as required. This change was complete by the end of 1811. Pasley's fieldworks training course at Plymouth was meanwhile proving successful and, coupled with Wellington's call for properly trained field engineers, resulted in a Royal Warrant dated 23 April 1812. This authorized the formation of the Royal

The Royal Military Canal.

General Sir Charles Pasley, KCB.

Engineer Establishment at Chatham to instruct the Royal Military Artificers and the junior officers of the Royal Engineers in sapping, mining and other military field-works. Pasley was promoted to Major and appointed the first Commandant. The transformation was further extended on 4 August 1812 when the Master General of the Ordnance ordered that the Royal Military Artificers be styled 'The Royal Military Artificers, or Sappers and Miners'. However, this more martial designation proved too cumbersome, and on 6 March 1813 the simpler title of 'Royal Sappers and Miners' was authorized.

Pasley's name lives on at Chatham, where the main thoroughfare through Brompton Barracks is called Pasley Road, and the Commandant of the Royal School of Military Engineering, who is 'double-hatted' as Commander, Chatham Garrison, lives in Pasley House.

In the winter of 1812/13, Wellington prepared his next advance to drive the French beyond the Pyrenees. Four compa-nies of the transformed Royal Sappers and Miners had been concentrated and a fifth was newly arrived. Nicknamed 'Pasley's Cadets' by the blue-uniformed engineer veterans of previous Peninsular battles, the new company had been trained recently at Chatham and equipped with scarlet coats, introduced so as not to be mistaken for Frenchmen by other units of the British army. Curiously, none of the new units had received training in musketry, and they were not equipped with weapons until 1817.

The assault on San Sebastian proved the value of the new training system, not only in siege warfare but also in bridging, where, in some of the bridging operations, the rival Royal Staff Corps gave valuable and gallant assistance. After numerous defeats, the French were driven from Portugal and Spain, and Napoleon was exiled to the island of Elba, between Corsica and the mainland of Italy. In 1815 he escaped, quickly formed another army and advanced into Belgium only to meet his final defeat near Brussels at the Battle of Waterloo on 18 June. Although there were ten Royal Sappers and Miners companies in Welling-ton's area of operations in the Low Coun-tries, there was no complete unit of the Royal Sappers and Miners present at Water-loo, which was mainly an infantry and cavalry encounter.

Following his defeat, Napoleon was exiled again, this time to the island of St Helena in the South Atlantic. A company of the Royal Sappers and Miners were stationed there to strengthen the sea defences, and they were also employed in building a house for the ex-Emperor. Napoleon died in 1821, and at the time it was alleged that his demise was accelerated by arsenic in the wallpaper of his sitting room (presumably decorated by the Royal Sappers and Miners). He was buried in a stone vault built by two of the Royal Sappers and Miners tradesmen, but twenty years later his body was exhumed and taken to Paris, where it was placed in a specially constructed tomb completed in 1861.

It is of interest to note that Waterloo was one of the first battles for which a campaign medal was awarded to all ranks who were present, although the actual issue was made some years later. The example shown is from the Royal Engineers Museum collection. The medals as issued were suspended from an iron ring, which tended to rust and stain the wearer's uniform; so many officers had them modified to avoid this problem.

The Waterloo Medal.

RETRENCHMENT AND PEACE

The post-Waterloo *pax-Britannica* in Europe brought the usual post-conflict reductions in strength both of Royal Engineers and Royal Sappers and Miners. The first cut in August 1816 reduced companies by 25 men, and the final axe in 1819 reduced the Royal Engineers to 193 officers and the Royal Sappers and Miners to 12 companies, each of 62 men.

Both Corps continued to be employed around the world on active service and peaceful development of the burgeoning British Empire. Expeditions to America, Algiers, Spain, South Africa, Canada, China, India, South America, Syria, and help for the settlers in Australia and New Zealand all required engineer support. By 1838 the Royal Staff Corps had ceased to exist, and its officers were placed on half pay or replaced by Royal Engineer officers, the rank and file being transferred to companies of the Royal Sappers and Miners.

Accurate survey had become more important following the Battle of Culloden in 1746. A full survey of Scotland for military purposes at a scale of 1 inch to 1,000 yards was ordered by the Board of Ordnance, which led to the creation of the Ordnance Survey in 1791. In 1824 the government decided to extend survey operations in Ireland with six inches to one mile mapping to complete map coverage of the British Isles. A special Survey Company was raised and trained at Pasley's Royal Engineer Establishment at Chatham. With a strength of 62, it was to be numbered the 13th Company, and two more, the 14th and 16th, quickly followed in 1825.

Three further companies were raised for general service in 1827, the 17th for service in Bermuda and the 18th and 19th for service in Canada. These were eventually responsible for the founding of Ottawa and the building of the Rideau Canal. However, these increases were followed by reductions in 1833, this time to 12 companies each of 91 men, nine for general service and three for survey.

Throughout all this, developments were being made in techniques and equipment, and the Royal Engineer Establishment took these into account as well as continuing to experiment with, and develop, military techniques such as mining. Instruction at the Royal Engineer Establishment included field and siege works, barrack construction, pontooning, practical geometry and surveying. In 1826 officers of the Royal Engineers began to receive training in practical architecture. With the invention of a diving-suit in the late 1830s, diving and underwater work and demolition were also included. In 1850, in an early example of a harmonization drive, it was decided to move the Royal Engineer Depot from Wool-wich to Chatham and combine it with the Royal Engineer Establishment in order to exploit the advantage of the extension of the North Kent Railway to Chatham.

The First Afghan War lasted from 1838 to 1842 and was fought because the British wished to install a puppet ruler on the throne of Afghanistan. Three engineering episodes stand out proudly in a war of blunders.

To launch the war, Bengal Engineers had to build a bridge across the River Indus. They then blew in the gates of the fortified city of Ghazni, supervised by Lieutenant Henry Durand, RE, and finally had to fortify the city of Jalalabad to check further Afghan advances into India. In the final retreat from Kabul, the invading force was annihilated in the passes of the Hindu Kush, where all but one man perished.

To close this period of history, we return to 10 July 1832, when King William IV (1830–7) granted 'to the Royal Regiment of Artillery and the Corps of Royal Engineers,

The Fortress of Ghazni.

His Majesty's permission to wear on their appointments the Royal Arms and Supporters, together with a cannon and the motto "Ubique quo fas et gloria ducunt".' Translated, this motto means 'Everywhere where right and glory lead'. The cannon survived as part of the Royal Engineers badge until 1868, when the Corps was relieved of the responsibility for constructing gun platforms for the Royal Artillery.

THE CRIMEAN WAR

Nearly forty years of relative peace in Europe that followed the Battle of Waterloo came to an end in 1854 with the outbreak of the Crimean War. The Sultan of Turkey had refused certain demands by the Tsar of Russia, so Russian troops invaded Turkey. Great Britain was anxious that Russia should not gain access to the Mediterranean Sea, so she allied with Turkey, France and Sardinia against the Russian aggression. This campaign became known as the Crimean War because it was on the Crimean peninsula that the army disembarked and where most of the actions were fought. It holds an important place in our history because it marked the ending of the era of siege warfare. (Not least of an abundance of changes was the fact that for the first time in a long while the French were our allies and not our enemies!)

The period of retrenchment after Waterloo had led to much stagnation in the army, and, as the Crimean campaign developed, outmoded procedures and serious deficiencies came to light. These were aggravated by the severity of the Russian winter, the effect of which had been drastically illustrated in previous campaigns and, indeed, has in more recent times. The hardships and privations endured by the

"What is a Sapper? This versatile genius ... condensing the whole system of military engineering and all that is useful and practical under one red jacket. He is a man of all work of the Army and the public – astronomer, geologist, surveyor, draughtsman, artist, architect, traveller, explorer, antiquary, mechanic, diver, soldier and sailor; ready to do anything or go anywhere; in short, he is a Sapper." – Captain T. W. J. Connolly, the historian of the Royal Sappers and Miners, 1855

troops were dramatically emphasized to the authorities and next-of-kin at home by two new inventions: photography and the telegraph. The Morse Code had been invented in 1832, and the first telegraph line ever used on active service was laid in the Crimea by the Royal Sappers and Miners. Reports from the front could therefore be received at home much more quickly than in previous campaigns, and the dreadful conditions rapidly became public knowledge. Indeed, the *Times* correspondent, W. H. Russell, made full use of the telegraph in dispatches to his paper in London. Realistic pictures could now also be made of the various scenes of war. Roger Fenton, an early exponent of this novel science of photography, made his way to the Crimea privately (and with some support from the Prince Consort). The results of these exposures were public outcry followed by action to rectify and reform, while some improvements were brought about by private initiative – Florence Nightingale and her work with the medical services is a well-known example. Alexis Soyer, a famous chef of the day, also went to the Crimea at his own expense in an attempt to improve catering in the field, and a version of his stove (the Soya Stove) is still in service today.

Nearly 100 Royal Engineer officers and 11 companies of Sappers and Miners took part in the campaign, and almost half the personnel involved became casualties. In addition to laying the telegraph line, their duties included constructing the first water-supply points, building a primitive railway, preparing a landing place at Balaclava and supervising working parties. The usual siegeworks occupied much of their attention. British earthworks and fortifications were under constant Russian gunfire, so the Sappers were in demand not only to repair damage and beat off attacks but to provide guides for the infantry moving up through the maze of trenches and saps to the front line. 'Follow the Sapper – quick march!' became a common order, as indeed it also was when the time came for the assault on Russian positions, the Sappers leading the way with their scaling ladders as they had done in previous campaigns.

The Crimean War saw not only campaign medals being issued (with bars for particular battles) but also the inception of the Victoria Cross as the supreme recognition of valour in the face of the enemy. It was, and still is, made from the bronze of melted-down Russian cannon captured during the Crimea campaign and is awarded regardless of rank. Three officers of the Royal Engineers and five Sappers and Miners were awarded the Victoria Cross during the Crimea campaign.

Two other events of great significance to the Corps occurred during this campaign.

The Redan in the Crimea.

First, on 25 May 1855, the Board of Ordnance was abolished. This long-overdue reform ended the 'private-army' status and at last brought the Artillery and Engineers under the command of the Commander-in-Chief and under the control of the War Office. Second, on 17 October 1856, the Royal Sappers and Miners were amalgamated with the Officers of the Royal Engineers to be known thereafter as the Corps of Royal Engineers. The long-standing anomaly of the officers and men belonging to separate Corps was now ended, and as a consequence the rank of the private engineer soldier was changed to Sapper. The depot of the old Royal Sappers and Miners was also moved in 1856 from Woolwich to Chatham, concentrating with the Royal Engineers Officers' Depot and the Royal Engineer Establishment to create a centre of Sapper excellence. Major General Whitworth Porter, a famous Corps historian, wrote: 'It speaks wonders for the good sense and fidelity of the Sappers and Miners that they were under such circumstances so invariably loyal to their officers. This difficulty is now at an end. Officers and men who had long considered themselves one Corps were, for the future, officially recognized as such.'

YEARS OF DEVELOPMENT AND SMALL WARS

Queen Victoria had been on the throne for only 19 of the 64 years of her long reign when the Crimean War ended in 1856. The end of the war led into a period that marked the zenith of the British Empire and brought a flood of new inventions. Throughout this period of spectacular change and development, the now-unified Royal Engineers were to play a very full part. This was not only because Sappers of all ranks were inevitably involved in the development of new machines and new techniques for both military and peaceful use, but many Royal Engineer officers were to become governors or senior administrators in parts of the expanding Empire.

First, however, came the Indian Mutiny. India was still governed by the East India Company, originally a trading organization, which maintained its own army of European and native troops. In the early part of the 19th century the pioneer units in the East India Company had been formed into three Corps of Sappers and Miners (which still exist today): Bengal in 1819, Bombay in 1826 and Madras in 1834. In 1857, some parts of the East India Company's army became discontented over certain events and conditions of service; they mutinied, committed numerous atrocities against Europeans and were eventually engaged in several bloody actions. At the relief of Delhi in 1857, two Bengal Engineer officers and a sergeant from the Bengal Sappers won the Victoria Cross. A further four Victoria Crosses were to be won by Engineers before the end of the mutiny.

*"The Lord, He created the Engineer,
Her Majesty's Royal Engineer,
With the rank and pay of a Sapper."*
— Kipling

The mutiny was suppressed with considerable vigour, and the outcome was that the government of India passed from the East India Company to the Crown. The transfer included its army, and thus the famous Indian Army came into being. The British officers and non-commissioned officers of the Company's Corps of Engineers were absorbed into the Corps of Royal Engineers in 1862, starting a connection that was to last for 85 years. Until independence, when Muslim Pakistan split from Hindu India in 1947, Royal Engineer officers and senior non-commissioned officers continued to be seconded to the engineer units of the Indian Army. The East India Company Engineers had a remarkable record, not only as military engineers but also in peaceful development, such as roads, irrigation schemes, survey and other civil works – which is a history in itself. This was to continue until independence.

Various small wars were now breaking out all over the Empire (which now covered almost one-quarter of the world's surface) or in areas of British interest, and the forces committed by the Government all needed engineer support. In 1860 an Expeditionary Force was sent to China to enforce the Treaty of Tientsin. The Force's 2nd Division was commanded by General Robert Napier, a Bengal Engineer who had commanded an Engineer Brigade in the final assault on Lucknow during the Indian Mutiny. He was given the mission of capturing the heavily fortified Taku Forts, which was successfully achieved with support from three companies of Royal Engineers and two companies of Madras Sappers and Miners. The victory at Taku led to the capture of Tientsin and Peking.

The RE units deployed to India and China were deficient in effective equipment and transport, but changes in establishments and improvements in equipment started to improve matters, and companies were converted to a permanent establishment. The 23rd, or Driver, Company was converted into a permanent train consisting of a Pontoon Troop, equipped with a semi-decked pontoon that lasted, with progressive modifications, until the end of the Great War in 1918, and a Field Equipment Troop. The latter was designed to carry the initial scales of tools and stores to support a 10,000-strong force supported by three Field Companies and a Field Park Company. It was the precursor of the updated equipment establishment of the new Field Companies that first saw action in the Zulu War.

The Abyssinia Campaign of 1867–8 was brought about by the refusal of the Abyssinian king to release several British prisoners including our ambassador. It has been said this was essentially a Royal Engineer's war. First, the force commander was Sir Robert Napier, the first engineer officer to command British forces in the field. Second, the country was rugged and underdeveloped, and the primary objective, the capital, Magdala, needed serious civil-engineering effort to reach it. This included constructing landing-piers on the coast, building roads inland and sinking wells along the routes, a 16-kilometre railway including eight girder bridges, and telegraph installations. Flag signalling was used for the first time in the army, as was photography. The work was aggravated by the mountainous country, which rose from sea level to 2,255 metres. The 10th

Company Royal Engineers and seven companies of Indian Sappers and Miners were required for the operation. When Magdala was reached, the king refused to surrender, so the artillery bombarded the town and the Sappers blew in one of the town gates. The defenders fled, leaving the king, who committed suicide. The British prisoners were released, and Sir Robert Napier was made Lord Napier of Magdala.

The Ashanti War of 1873 also proved to be very much an engineer operation in support of the infantry force. Royal Engineers built some 200 kilometres of roads through swamp and jungle as well as constructing numerous bridges and pioneering the use of static steam-engines as winches and engineer construction plant. The Corps was also involved in subsequent Ashanti Wars in 1895 and 1900.

In 1878 the Second Afghan War was fought in a further attempt to control the rebellious country and, in contrast to the first campaign, was well planned and executed. Some 167 officers and 18 companies of Sappers took part. Sappers bridged the Kabul River many times, constructed fortified posts, laid telegraph lines, built railways and mapped the country. Lieutenant Thomas Rice Henn, RE, and a party of Bombay Sappers were the last to leave the line of battle at Maiwand, and on 29 July 1880, having made a final stand to cover the retreat, died at their posts, to the fear and admiration of the enemy. This led to General Roberts's march from Kabul and the Battle of Kandahar, which ended the war in 1880.

Egypt and neighbouring Sudan then assumed some prominence. Since 1517, Egypt had been part of the Ottoman Empire and was ruled by the Khedive on behalf of the Turkish sultan. In 1869 the Suez Canal was opened, affording a shorter route from Europe to India and the Far East, a considerable advantage to Great Britain and her Empire. The Suez Canal had been built by a Frenchman, Ferdinand de Lesseps, the French having leased the land through which the canal was constructed. The Khedive had borrowed large sums of money from France and Great Britain, but it appeared that there was little chance of his repaying the loans. France and Great Britain therefore took over 'Dual Financial Control' of Egypt, which naturally proved unpopular with its people and led to unrest. France withdrew from this arrangement, leaving Britain to rule Egypt and the Sudan alone.

A revolt broke out in 1882, and the government dispatched an expeditionary force, which reached Ismailia on the banks of the Suez Canal. The force, commanded by Major General Graham, RE, who had won the Victoria Cross in the Crimea, then marched across the desert to defeat the rebels at Kassassin. The main Royal Engineer involvement was the erection of a telegraph line simultaneously with the advance, while the newly formed 8th Railway Company controlled and maintained the railway and ran the trains. It is of interest that this was the first time that the Commander British Forces was able to report his victory directly to London from the field.

The British were now practically the rulers of Egypt and had interests in the Sudan. In 1884 Sudanese tribes led by a religious fanatic called the Mahdi revolted. To relieve Egyptian garrisons in the Sudan, a

26th Field Company embarked on the River Nile.

force was sent under Major General Charles Gordon, an ingenious and charismatic Sapper officer, highly experienced in defensive works. However, he was besieged in Khartoum by the Mahdi's dervishes before he was able to complete the evacuation of the garrison. In 1885 a relief force was sent up the Nile to relieve Gordon but was delayed because the boats could not negotiate the rapids. They arrived just too late, Gordon having been killed on the palace steps only two days before, after a siege of ten and a half months.

A member of the relief force was another Sapper, Major Kitchener, who was also to become famous. He had already achieved some notoriety and, as a young officer, had surveyed the Holy Land and Cyprus. After the attempt to save Gordon he held a number of administrative posts in Egypt and by 1892 had become Commander-in-Chief, training and reorganizing the Egyptian Army for the reconquest of the Sudan and to avenge the death of Gordon. To maintain communications with Cairo, the now General Kitchener decided to cut across 370 kilometres of desert by extending the existing railway over unsurveyed terrain devoid of surface water. This involved pushing the enemy southwards a few miles at a time until the railway caught up, at the same time boring wells along the line of communication. Eventually the railway was laid as far as Berber, 240 kilometres farther than originally planned. Lieutenant Edouard Girouard, RE, a French Canadian-born officer who had been trained on the Canadian Pacific Railway, organized this work; he was to achieve further fame and a knighthood for railway work in later campaigns. He was one of a total of 125 Canadians from the

Royal Military College, Kingston, Ontario, who were to be commissioned into the Corps over the years from 1880.

Kitchener made his final advance to Omdurman in 1898, where the Dervish enemy was finally defeated. Another point of interest is that taking part in the cavalry charge at the Battle of Omdurman was a young cavalry officer called Winston Churchill, later to become prime minister in the darkest days of 1940. The Sudan operation was also one of the first campaigns in which khaki uniform was worn.

The foregoing campaigns have been covered in some detail to show the types of operations being fought in the latter half of the 19th century and how engineer skills were needed in the progress of these campaigns. It also demonstrates that engineer officers, no less than officers of other branches of the army, could rise to command a force of all-arms in battle. It also recognized the triple utility of Royal Engineers:

First and foremost, they are soldiers, capable of fighting as fully trained infantrymen.

Second, they are Sappers with expertise in all aspects of field engineering.

Third, they are tradesmen with all the skills necessary to enhance the general and civil engineering capability of the Corps.

The titles of all Corps trades, whatever their persuasion, are prefixed with the term 'Military Engineer'.

In 1869 the title of the Royal Engineer Establishment at Chatham was changed to The School of Military Engineering, to

The Prah River, Ashanti.

reflect its status as one of the leading military scientific schools in Europe. As one of these institutions, the school was at the forefront of testing and adapting new equipment and technology for military use, including mechanical transport, balloons and kites, electrically controlled sea mines, torpedoes and searchlights. The range of courses then taught at Chatham included instruction in:

Ballooning
Bridging
Demolitions
Electricity and telegraphy
Electric light in field operations
Engine driving
Estimating and building construction
Field fortifications
Fitting and turning
Lithography (printing)
Modelmaking
Photography and chemistry
Railways
Siegeworks and mining
Stoking and management of steam boilers
Survey
Submarine mining
Woodworking machinery

These skills were learnt and put into practice by Sappers of all ranks. When not campaigning or improving defences, work was going on in most parts of the British Empire, opening up and developing countries by means of road-building, bridge, canal, railway and dam construction, as well as irrigation schemes and telegraph networks. Additionally the Royal Engineers assisted the administration of the Empire by conducting surveys and boundary commissions, and with geological and archaeological exploration.

Royal Engineer officers were employed as governors in New Zealand, Hong Kong, East Africa and Malta, and one even became Burgomaster of Johannesburg. Of other notable officers, Captain Francis Fowke, RE, became well known in architectural circles, including involvement in the design of the Natural History Museum in South Kensington and the Royal Albert Hall. Unfortunately he died in 1865 from overwork, and Major General Scott completed the Royal Albert Hall. In his memory the Fowke Medal in bronze is awarded to the best student on Clerk of Works (Construction) Courses. Perhaps not quite so well known is Major Sir Francis Marindin, RE, one of seven enthusiasts who set up the Football Association in 1871. The Corps won the FA Cup in 1875, even with an all-officer team!

Further change was meanwhile happening in the army as a whole. In 1870, far-reaching reforms were announced by the Secretary of State for War, Edward Cardwell. These reforms heralded changes to the army's structure as well as alterations to its conditions and terms of service. For soldiers, one of the main changes was enlistment for 12 years' regular service – previously enlistment had been for 21 years, and many units were composed of soldiers who were very much 'beyond the first flush of youth' and unfit for the rigours of field service. Later, the 12 years were split between a number of years of active service with the Colours and the balance in the Reserve: seven and five was a common split, and the principle remains extant to this day.

WAR IN SOUTH AFRICA, A CAP BADGE AND A SONG

While the Corps continued to keep abreast of modern developments in military engineering, political unrest also continued, particularly in southern Africa, which had been colonized by both the British and the Boers (who were of Dutch origin). Trouble flared up first in 1879 with the native Zulus. Although regarded by Europeans as savages, they were in fact socially highly sophisticated, with a strong military ethos, very well organized, trained and disciplined. Under their King Cetshwayo, they resented European colonization in Africa, and tension rose, particularly with the Boers, who both suffered and committed atrocities. Eventually, the British took the initiative and marched four columns, which included the 2nd, 5th, 7th and 30th Companies RE, into Zululand. With complacent arrogance, the British underestimated the Zulus, who inflicted a total defeat on a British column at Isandlwana, killing three-quarters of an 1,800-strong force. Colonel Anthony Durnford, RE, lost his life leading a covering force protecting the withdrawal of the main column. The day after the disaster, 22 January 1879, a few miles south at Rorke's Drift, Lieutenant John Chard, RE, of the 5th Company was to win a Victoria Cross, one of 11 awarded that day. Being a year senior to the infantry commander, he assumed command of a mixed force based on B Company of the 2nd Battalion, 24th Regiment (South Wales Borderers). The attacking Zulu force, estimated at 4,000 warriors newly equipped with Lee Metford rifles taken from the dead of Isandlwana and highly confident, were bloodily repulsed in an epic defensive operation. Later in the year the Zulus were finally defeated and their king exiled.

But peace was not to last long before another short war started, this time against the Dutch settlers in southern Africa. This First Boer War, which lasted from 1880 to 1881, was fought because the British were dissatisfied with Boer administration in the Transvaal and annexed it in order to govern it properly. It was a messy little war, fought out between the pious but militarily effective Boers and a poorly led and generally ineffective British army amongst the townships, plains and hills of the Transvaal. Discovery of gold on the Rand in 1886, together with exploitation of the Kimberley diamond fields, especially by British miners, aggravated the situation. The Boers wanted to oust the British, who in turn were determined to stay. The clash came with the start of a second Boer War in 1899 which lasted until 1902. The British had not learned the lessons of the previous campaign. Despite superior equipment and organization, they suffered many early setbacks because they were slow-moving, cumbersome, and accustomed to small colonial wars usually against a less well-equipped enemy. Some

> *"When you've shouted*
> *Rule Britannia,*
> *When you've sung God*
> *Save the Queen – When*
> *you've finished killing*
> *Kruger with your*
> *mouth,*
> *Will you kindly drop a*
> *shilling in my little*
> *tambourine?*
> *For a gentleman in*
> *khaki, ordered South"*
> — Kipling

Steam Sapper No 8 at Chatham,

450,000 British and Empire troops were involved against some 90,000 Boers, the first occasion since Napoleonic times that Britain had been involved in a war on this scale.

The Boers engaged in what is now regarded as guerrilla warfare. They knew the country, were adept at concealment through hunting and stalking game, were very accurate shots, quick-witted and cunning. Furthermore, every man was mounted and highly mobile; he wore no recognizable uniform so that, if necessary, he could easily melt away into the non-combatant population. These bands of Boers were known as 'commandos', a term that was to be resurrected forty years later in another war. Through early setbacks, particularly in the area of medical treatment and field health, defeats and the occasional victory, the British slowly identified the key lessons. They were assisted by other colonials from the Dominions of Canada, Australia and New Zealand, who all contributed troops, as did loyal South Africans of British ancestry. Eventually, a large part of the British infantry was used in a mounted, and very mobile, role. The employment of barbed-wire fences and blockhouses to prevent free movement gradually restricted the Boers and allowed the British army to bring its combat power to bear. The Royal Navy was also prominent with landing parties manning guns taken from warships and mounted on field carriages. A peace settlement was agreed in 1902, and the Union of South Africa came into being.

In the Second Boer War, the Royal Engineers expanded considerably and the following types of units were employed:

Field Companies – employed mostly on defence works, construction of batteries, magazines, and light bridges

Balloon Sections – to observe enemy movement and to direct artillery fire

Bridging Battalions – to construct pontoon and heavy bridges

Telegraph Divisions – for signals communication

Railway Battalions – to repair railway track and to run and control trains

Searchlight and Survey Sections – to provide illumination and ground survey/maps

Left: Queen's South Africa Medal.
Right: King's South Africa Medal.

Road Transport Companies – to run steam traction engines known as 'Steam Sappers'

The Royal Engineers were also represented in the higher command, where Major General Lord Kitchener, who had become Baron Kitchener of Khartoum in 1898 after victory in the Sudan, was appointed Chief of Staff in 1900, and later became overall Force Commander.

The South African War was also the first in which all ranks were clothed in a khaki field service dress. With this change in military fashion the Corps also received its first cap badge, the design setting the style for the present pattern. The troops also brought back with them the Corps song, 'Hurrah for the CRE', which is still sung at Corps' occasions today. The words, which are largely Zulu in origin, can be found on page 132.

MODERNIZATION

After the poor performance in the Boer War, new lessons had to be identified and then applied. It was not acceptable to the Government and the British military establishment that the army of the most powerful nation in the world had been taught a savage lesson in the field by amateur soldiers made up of Boer farmers. However, political considerations also applied because the growth of the British

Empire had been watched enviously by other countries. France and Germany also had overseas colonies and were rapidly catching up with industrialized Britain. They also wished to extend their influence by expansion and had watched Britain's problems in South Africa with a certain degree of satisfaction – indeed, both countries had given assistance to the Boers. The growing military strength of other nations, particularly Germany, and the growing possibility of a European war called for political as well as military reforms. In an attempt to end British isolation from the rest of Europe, an alliance with France was made in 1904 – the so-called 'Entente Cordiale'.

Within the army, reforms were initiated in 1904 by Richard Haldane, the Minister for War. The most notable were:

The post of Commander-in-Chief was abolished and replaced by the Army Council, which continues today as the Executive Committee of the Army Board.

A General Staff was formed and linked with Canada, Australia, New Zealand, and the new Union of South Africa, being renamed the Imperial General Staff.

The War Office was reorganized into early defined departments with specific responsibilities.

The Regular Army at home was divided into geographical commands for peacetime administration.

The Reserve Army was completely reorganized as an extension of the Regular Army and renamed the Territorial Force.

The Staff College and its courses were enlarged and extended.

On a more personal note for the soldier, in 1902 khaki serge uniform, more suitable for the European climate, was introduced. This was to be the combat uniform for the whole army. In 1908 Mills-Burrows web infantry equipment was also introduced, the first scientifically designed load-carrying equipment for the soldier and the Short Magazine Lee-Enfield rifle came into general service. With this strong, reliable and accurate weapon, the British soldier attained a reputation for rapid and accurate fire, and in its various marks this rifle was to remain in service for over fifty years. The end product of these reforms was troops who were well equipped, could shoot accurately and rapidly, and could use ground to the best advantage.

The Corps was very much part of all this modernization and changes can be summarized as follows:

Aviation. The Corps set up a School of Ballooning and a balloon factory near Aldershot in 1892 (the use of balloons on active service in South Africa has already been mentioned). Further experiments continued with improved balloons, man-lifting kites and airships. In 1903, the Wright Brothers in America made the first flight in a heavier-than-air machine, and the new science of aviation expanded rapidly. In 1905 the balloon factory moved to Farnborough and in 1909

"For it's Tommy this, an' Tommy that, an' chuck him out, the brute. But it's Saviour of 'is Country when the guns begin to shoot" – Kipling

Filling a balloon at Aldershot.

came under civilian control; it continues today as the Royal Aerospace Establishment. Lieutenant Rex Cammell, RE, made the first official military flight in an aeroplane in 1910. It is also of interest to note that the first military use of ground-to-air radio was in 1911, when a message was sent to an airship 48 kilometres away by a Royal Engineers Signals unit. Also in 1911 the Balloon School was reorganized as the Air Battalion RE, and in 1912 it became a separate Corps as the Royal Flying Corps (Naval and Military Wing). From this early beginning emerged, in 1918, the Royal Air Force and the Fleet Air Arm.

Submarine Mining. With the Royal Navy's introduction of steam propulsion to replace sail, stronger defences for harbours were needed in the shape of underwater mines, coastal-defence searchlights and coastal artillery. Apart from gunnery, experiments, which included diving, had been going on for some time at the School of Military Engineering, so it was decided in 1871 that the Royal Engineers would form Submarine Mining Companies. These flourished and expanded, being equipped with the Brennan Torpedo in 1887, which the Corps manufactured and operated. This was the first underwater guided weapon, and it had potential for attack as well as defence. In 1905 it was decided that the Submarine Mining Companies should be disbanded and their duties handed over to the Royal Navy. It is interesting to note that it was about this time that the first practical submarine boats were being introduced by the Royal Navy and other navies.

Mechanical Transport. The use of steam traction-engines or 'Steam Sappers' in South Africa has already been mentioned – in fact, the 45th Company was raised especially for this purpose. These machines had many other uses as static power-plants for workshops and mobile searchlights, and for hauling the heavy hydrogen-gas bottles for ballooning. But there was increasing interest in mechanical

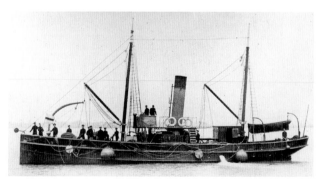

The Royal Engineers minelayer ship, General Skinner.

34

transport as the internal combustion engine began to develop, and a War Office Committee was set up to consider military applications. In 1902 they decided that mechanical transport for the army should become the responsibility of the Army Service Corps. The first Mechanical Transport Companies were formed in 1903/4 and trained by Royal Engineer instructors. Thereafter, up to 1914, the whole responsibility was gradually transferred from the Royal Engineers to the Army Service Corps.

THE GREAT WAR

> *"We have not always agreed, but having been under your displeasure as a subaltern, I shall always look back with satisfaction to having been your colleague."*
> – Churchill to Kitchener, 1915

The conflicting interests of the great powers of Europe came to a climax in 1914, with two powerful opposing alliances emerging. The Central Powers, consisting initially of Germany and Austria-Hungary, was later joined by Turkey. The other alliance was the Triple Entente of Great Britain, France and Russia. In addition, the majority of non-aligned countries in Europe had been rearming because of a growing fear of both Germany and the problem of Austro-Hungarian influence in the Balkans resulting from the decay of the Turkish Empire.

The shooting of the Austrian Archduke Franz Ferdinand by a Serbian assassin was the match that set Europe alight. The Austro-Hungarian Empire, backed by Germany, declared war on Serbia. Russia then mobilized to protect Serbia, and Germany, in accordance with its alliance with Austria-Hungary, declared war on Russia. Putting into effect its long-standing plan based on a two-front war scenario, Germany launched an attack on France, invading via Belgium without warning and causing Great Britain and the Empire to declare war on Germany on 4 August 1914. This was the beginning of a wide-ranging conflict, with many other nations taking part. The war was originally called the Great War and, after the end of the Second World War, was also referred to as the First World War. The main theatres of war on land were:

The **Western Front**, the main theatre, where Britain with her Dominions, together with France, Belgium and, later, Portugal, fought the Germans. In April 1917 the Allies were joined by the USA.

The **Eastern Front**. Here Russia fought against Germany and the Austro-Hungarians until 1917, when the Communist Revolution caused Russia to drop out of the war.

In **Italy**, the Italians fought against the Austro-Hungarians, later assisted by Britain.

In the **Middle East**, Britain and her Dominions fought Turkey (aided by Germany) and entered Palestine in a campaign to prevent the Turks and Germans seizing the Suez Canal.

The Balkans, where Britain, France, Serbia, Romania and Greece fought against Austria-Hungary, Turkey and Bulgaria.

In Africa, the colonial powers of Britain and Germany fought each other, mainly in Germany's African territories.

It was fortunate for the British army that the reforms instituted after the South African War were just beginning to take effect when war was declared in 1914. However, the reform's aim of producing mobile troops able to use ground was thwarted on the Western Front when, by the end of 1914, the two opposing armies had started to dig extensive trench systems for a static war of position that was to last nearly four years.

That most famous of engineer officers, Field Marshal Lord Kitchener, had become Secretary of State for War and was the brains behind the expansion of the army. The so-called 'Kitchener's New Armies' were formed from an initial mass influx of enthusiastic volunteers. Kitchener himself was drowned in 1916 en route to Russia in HMS *Hampshire* when the cruiser hit a mine in the Pentland Firth, near Scapa Flow, and sank.

In 1914 the British Regular Army went to war with two field companies of Royal Engineers in each infantry division (later increased to three) and one field squadron with the cavalry division, just over 12,000 all ranks. Two fortress companies, to carry out what we now understand as force engineering, were sent to operate on the line of communication. In August 1914, the total strength of the Royal Engineers, both Regular army and Territorial Force, was

25,000 in 205 units. At the end in 1918 the corresponding figure, excluding transportation, was 230,000 in 1,832 units – a proportionally greater increase than any other corps in the army. This huge expansion saw a corresponding increase in the various types of units dealing with advances in science and technology for military purposes and the wide variety of campaigns in various theatres of war. Yet, like their forebears leading assaulting parties with scaling-ladders in the Napoleonic and Crimean Wars, Royal Engineer units were invariably used for consolidating gains, particularly in the closely entrenched positions on the Western Front. Acting as close support to the assaulting infantry, the Sappers were often required to fight and then use their engineering skills to consolidate the new position. Very many instances of extreme gallantry were recorded in these actions.

The Corps was also very much concerned with the expansion of military capability. Particularly on the Western Front, Royal Engineer field companies were fully occupied in the manufacture and installation of all sorts of fixtures and fittings to enable troops to live and fight in the extensive trench system. Pumps were required to keep the excavations as dry as possible, and light railway systems were installed to move men and material from the rear areas. The art of camouflage was also developed to mislead the enemy. Forestry companies were formed to harvest, treat and cut the vast amounts of timber required for trench revetment, pit props, bridging and hutting. In order to sustain the army, camps, stores depots, workshops and all manner of buildings and

Major Peter Nissen and the hut he designed.

associated services were required, and many works service units had to be raised to carry out work that civilian contractors would have done in peacetime. A particular capability was the hut designed by Captain Nissen, RE, in 1916. This semicircular corrugated-iron hut was a simple, easily and rapidly erected structure that solved countless accommodation problems. Examples of the Nissen hut can still be seen today, and the current temporary accommodation system uses a similar hooped-frame system. An example of a large project in direct support of the fighting troops was the construction of a pipeline across the Sinai Desert to deliver filtered Nile water to British troops during the Palestine campaign.

The Western Front brought miners to the fore again. A feature of the static nature of this front was that the trench system could not be outflanked, so both sides dug tunnels under enemy positions. When explosives in those planted beneath German positions on Vimy Ridge were fired, the explosion was heard in London. The tunnelling companies' finest moments included the mines exploded on 1 July 1916 in support of the Somme attack; while perhaps the greatest achievement of all was on 7 June 1917 on the Messines-Wytschaete Ridge, when mines totalling 450 tonnes of ammonal blew the Germans off the feature as part of the opening moves in the Third Battle of Ypres, affording a tactical victory for the British and Dominion forces at minimal human cost.

Telegraph and wireless, or radio, technology advanced quickly during the Great War, and the Royal Engineers Signal Service expanded from 31 to 531 units (this including carrier-pigeon and messenger-dog units). Likewise, the original five Railway Companies expanded into a Transportation Service of 100,000 men who not only built and operated railways but also operated docks, ports, coastal craft and inland-water transport. Included in this capability was the Movement Control Service, which in effect ran an enormous railway and shipping organization.

Apart from normal military mapping requirements, there was a demand for accurate mapping of gun and target positions, bringing increased importance to the Military Survey Branch. The Ordnance Survey, although really the national mapmaking institution of Great Britain, also played a part in what became a vast undertaking, and during the war some 43 million maps of all sorts were issued.

But it was not only expansion that affected the Corps. New inventions and the exploitation of existing technologies were by now part of the Corps' normal duties, and one of its new responsibilities was chemical warfare. In April 1915 a German gas attack against the Canadians and French Colonial troops at Ypres, in Belgium, took the Allies by surprise, and it was only a month later that the British Government decided to retaliate in kind. Major C. H. Foulkes, DSO, RE, was appointed to exploit the use of gas and to organize, train and direct the specially raised Special Brigade RE. The first British gas attack on the enemy was in September 1915 at Loos.

The development of the aeroplane for military use led to the need for searchlights to illuminate enemy aircraft so that they could be located and attacked by anti-aircraft artillery. As the Corps was already responsible for coastal-defence searchlights, this also became a Sapper responsibility. However, a new dimension was added to aerial warfare when an aircraft dropped bombs into the sea off Dover in December 1914, and the first real air raids by Zeppelin airships began in January 1915. By the end of the war, 629 searchlights were deployed in the UK alone.

The Corps also pioneered armoured warfare. It was Lieutenant Colonel E. D. Swinton, RE, who first suggested in 1914 the practical concept of an armoured fighting vehicle – its armour plate and ability to move on caterpillar tracks being a means to overcome the trench stalemate and the high casualty rate from enemy machine-guns and barbed-wire on the Western Front. Trials took place in 1916 and the vehicles were given the deception name of 'tanks' to make the enemy believe that they were to be used for water supply. The name stuck. These new weapons were to be operated by the Heavy Section Machine Gun Corps, which in 1917 became the Tank Corps. Although it was not a direct descendant of a Royal Engineers unit, many Royal Engineers officers were involved in the development of the tank and the subsequent evolution of the Tank Corps. Brigadier Elles was one of the first commanders, and Major (later Lieutenant General Sir Giffard) Martel was prominent in later development. Major

A Mark I Male Tank.

A Tankette.

General Sir John Capper, who had earlier been prominent in the Royal Flying Corps, became Director General of the Tank Corps in 1917.

With Russia out of the war in 1917, the Allies gaining the upper hand in the Balkans and Middle East, and the arrival in France of a young, vibrant and ever-expanding United States army, it became obvious that the outcome of the war would be decided on the Western Front. In March 1918 the Germans, in a final attempt to win the war before American matériel and manpower resources became decisive, mounted a ferocious offensive against the Allies called the *Kaiserschlacht* or the 'Kaiser's Battle'. The aim was to drive a wedge between the French and British and capture Paris and the Channel ports. They came within a whisker of succeeding, and the Allies beat them back with great difficulty. By August, however, the Allies had begun to get the upper hand and, despite huge casualties on both sides, gradually started to push the German army back to a homeland that had all but collapsed into political turmoil and starvation. After four long, hard years of static warfare, mobile operations restarted until an Armistice was agreed on 11 November 1918.

The Treaty of Versailles in 1919 formally brought the Great War to an end. It can be argued that its provisions were so severe on the Germans that the induced rancour merely postponed another war for twenty years. A British Army of Occupation was stationed in Germany on the Rhine around Cologne until 1926, when it moved to Wiesbaden until 1929.

Twenty Victoria Crosses were awarded to Sappers during the Great War, but only 16 of these were to individuals in Royal Engineers units. Two were awarded to Royal New Zealand Engineers and one to a Royal Canadian Engineer. Major Edward 'Mick' Mannock was seconded from the Corps to what had become the Royal Air Force in 1918 when he was awarded the Victoria Cross. He was one of the air aces of the war and had already been awarded the Distinguished Service Order and two bars, and the Military Cross and bar.

A TROUBLED PEACE

At the end of the Great War there was almost immediate general demobilization of conscript soldiers and the usual post-war retrenchment and economies in the Regular army. In 1922 some of the reductions in the cavalry and infantry were achieved by amalgamation of regiments, and there was a corresponding reduction in the number of Royal Engineer units. However, the British army was still required to keep the peace throughout the Empire and elsewhere where our interests or treaty obligations prevailed.

In Russia, British troops, which had first been sent to Russia in 1917 to support the White, or Nationalist, Russians against the Communist, or Red, Russians were involved in some fighting but were withdrawn in 1919. The Middle East area continued to be a cauldron. In Afghanistan, a jihad was declared against the British in 1919, against the background of civil disturbance in India, and attacks were made in the areas of the Khyber Pass, Baluchistan, Waziristan and eastern Persia. The uprising was not fully quelled until 1925, and a consequence was that the Khyber Railway was constructed to enable reliable logistic support for future operations. In Iraq, Britain held a mandate to protect that country after the Great War, but in 1920 the Arabs revolted and 60,000 British and Indian troops took five months to subdue them. The engineer units involved were all from the Indian Sappers and Miners with Royal Engineer officers.

Egypt had been recognized as an independent state since 1922, but Britain retained a garrison for external defence, primarily to protect the Suez Canal, and retained control of Sudan. This caused tensions, and the garrison had to deal with mutinous Sudanese troops and sporadic violence and rioting in Egypt. Tensions also existed between the Greeks and Turks, and a confrontation took place in 1922 over the displacement of Greeks until a negotiated settlement followed the sending of a force of British troops. In Cyprus, pro-Greek rioting occurred in 1931 and was quelled by the quick arrival of troops flown in from Egypt, the first instance of this deployment method being used. Palestine was another country in which Great Britain held a mandate. However, tension was growing between Arabs and Jews, and trouble broke out in 1929. Some measure of order was achieved until 1936, when the Arabs rose again, and two divisions of British troops were needed to keep the peace.

In the Far East, the Chinese civil war took an anti-foreign bias in 1927 and threatened the Treaty Ports. This in turn led to an operation to defend the International Settlement at Shanghai. Troops sent from Britain and India forestalled trouble and were withdrawn after about a year. In India, trouble on the North-West Frontier and in Afghanistan continued to be a regular occurrence, and various campaigns were fought against dissident tribesmen between 1919 and 1939. Engineer involvement was invariably by the Indian Sappers and Miners. In Africa the

The Khyber Railway under construction.

Abyssinian crisis was precipitated by Italy's invasion of that country in 1935, which caused a British force to be established outside Alexandria in Egypt. Rapidly erected accommodation and water-supply for a brigade outside the town was provided by 2nd Field Company. Two companies of searchlights were also involved in harbour protection.

Nearer to home, the centuries-old struggle for Irish independence had erupted again in 1916 as the Easter Rising, and it was not until 1921 that a truce was reached between the British and the rebels. This led to the 26 counties of the Irish Free State (Eire) becoming a self-governing Dominion in 1922, and the British garrison departed after two-hundred years. The six counties of Northern Ireland remained as a constituent part of the United Kingdom. It is of interest that, under the Treaty Ports clause of the settlement, Britain retained ports and anchorages in the Free State until 1938, with works support being provided by the Corps.

In all of these activities the Corps was represented either by resident units, usually the so-called Fortress Companies, or by units or individuals deployed from adjacent garrisons.

By the mid-1930s the Headquarters of the Corps had settled back at Chatham and remained there until the end of the decade.

Locations of units in the 1930s were:

School of Military Engineering – St Mary's Barracks
Depot Battalion Royal Engineers – Kitchener Barracks
Training Battalion Royal Engineers – Brompton Barracks

Other key parts of the Corps' training machine were located as follows:

RE Mounted Depot – Aldershot (for equitation training)
Railway Training Centre – Longmoor, near Aldershot
Experimental Bridging Company – Christchurch
Anti-aircraft Searchlight Battalion – Blackdown near Aldershot.

The headquarters of the Survey Battalion was at Southampton with subordinate Survey companies being based where required. 19 Field Survey Company also had a small training cadre, but Military Survey had been much reduced since 1918, and most of its personnel were employed within the Ordnance Survey.

From the very first Soldier-Artificer Company at Gibraltar, boys had been enlisted to be trained as drummers or artificers. This was still the case, and the Depot Battalion included a Boys Company. Boys were enlisted primarily as buglers but were also taught a trade before joining for adult service at the age of 18. In order to meet the challenge of technological advance within the army, it was decided to set up an Army Technical School (Boys) to train apprentices in a variety of trades. The school was set up in 1923 at Chepstow, and after a four-year course the newly qualified tradesmen were posted to an appropriate Corps. This scheme was a great success, and, since there was demand for even more tradesmen in the army, the War Office decided that each of the technical corps would have its own school. The Royal Engineers school was built in Gillingham and entitled Army Technical School (Boys), Fort Darland. Here training began at the start of 1939, also incorporating the Boys' Company from the Depot Battalion at Chatham. It is of interest to note that two Victoria Cross winners from the Great War, Captain James McCudden, VC, DSO, MC, MM, of the Royal Flying Corps and Captain Alfred Toye, VC, MC, of the Middlesex Regiment, had both started their military careers as Enlisted Boys in the Corps.

The march of technology saw other changes. The Royal Air Force had become a separate service after its Royal Engineer beginnings. Now it was the turn of the Royal Engineers Signal Service to gain independence, and in 1920 it was formed into a separate Corps that eventually became the Royal Corps of Signals.

Mechanization was also becoming prominent on two counts. Technical developments during the Great War were leading to the replacement of cavalry and horse-drawn transport in favour of motor vehicles. In 1927 a Directorate of Mechanization was set up in the War Office to conduct trials of vehicles and carry out other experiments. The trials unit was 17th Field Company, and this eventually become the first Mechanized Field Company in 1927. It was commanded by Major Martel, who was earlier involved in tank development. By 1938 he was a Brigadier and appointed Deputy Director of Mechanization at the War Office.

The second aspect of mechanization was the need to repair and maintain the increasing numbers of motor vehicles and technical equipment entering service. Various committees were set up to investigate this, and for some time it was mooted that the Royal Engineers should provide the mechanical engineers and workshops. The committees were still deferring their decision in 1939. The suppliers and users of the bulk of the vehicles, the Royal Army Ordnance Corps and the Royal Army Service Corps, continued the repair and maintenance service that they were already providing. The impasse was not finally resolved until 1942 when the Royal Electrical and Mechanical Engineers was formed. Artificers Royal Artillery and Mechanics from the Royal Army Service Corps and Royal Army Ordnance Corps were rebadged to form this Corps, but very few Royal Engineers were included, at least initially. Yet another committee had looked into anti-aircraft defence, and in 1938 it decided that responsibility for anti-aircraft and coast-defence searchlights should be gradually transferred to the Royal Artillery.

After the Great War, full-dress uniform for the troops was not reintroduced, except for Household Troops in London and regimental bands. Service dress thus became both the combat uniform and parade dress for the majority of the army. Some slight improvements were made, and in the Corps collar badges were introduced for other ranks in 1922. Officers had worn bronze collar badges from the introduction of the khaki uniform in 1902. In the mid-1930s experiments were being made with a looser-fitting combat uniform, and this was introduced in 1939 as battledress. At the same time a lighter and improved web equipment began to be issued. The soldier was still armed with the rifle with which he had fought the Great War and sundry campaigns since. A new light machine-gun was accepted into service in 1937 and was gradually issued to units. This weapon replaced the Lewis gun and was called the BREN (BR from the Czechoslovakian town of Brno where it was developed, and EN from the Royal Small Arms Factory Enfield where the British version was made).

THE SECOND WORLD WAR

Less than twenty years elapsed before the outbreak of a second major war in Europe. In 1933 Germany had become a National Socialist state under the democratically elected leadership of Adolf Hitler and his Nazi Party, whose doctrine was the pre-eminence of the German race, domination of neighbouring states and the abrogation of the conditions of the Treaty of Versailles imposed on Germany in 1919. Closely allied to Nazi Germany was Italy, now a Fascist state controlled by another dictator, Benito Mussolini, who, like Hitler, had territorial ambitions. Japan's policy was also expansionist, and the alliance of the three countries was called the Axis. Britain and France were concerned as to the intentions of the Axis, not only in Europe but also in the Middle and Far East, where they had colonies and diplomatic interests.

The Spanish Civil War, which started in 1936, provided indications of what a modern war would be like, in particular the impact of the development of air power and its use in support of armoured troops. The Axis powers took advantage of this conflict to develop new concepts and equipment, particularly the coordination of the all-arms battlefield. The German reoccupation of the Rhineland and the Italian invasion of Abyssinia, followed by the Nazi annexation of Austria and Czechoslovakia, led to the Munich Crisis of 1938. Rearma-

"The Sappers really need no tribute from me; their reward lies in the glory of their achievement. The more science intervenes in warfare, the more will be the need for engineers in the field armies; in the late war there were never enough Sappers at any time. Their special tasks involved the upkeep and repair of communications; roads, bridges, railways, canals, mine sweeping. The Sappers rose to great heights in World War II and their contribution to victory was beyond all calculations."
– Field Marshal Lord Montgomery, 1945

ment and general preparation for an impending war was now in top gear, and in July 1939, for the first time ever in peacetime, conscription was begun.

Despite a final warning from the Allies, Hitler invaded Poland on 1 September 1939. On 3 September, after a final ultimatum to Germany, Great Britain, followed by the Dominions and Empire, declared war on Germany. Poland was rapidly overcome. For a time the Allies and Germany faced each other in North-West Europe in what became known as 'the phoney war'. This came to an end with the German invasion of Denmark and Norway in April 1940, followed by Holland and Belgium in May. The invasion by the Germans was spearheaded by a combined-arms operation called *blitzkrieg*, or 'lightning war', whereby parachutists seized key points while armoured forces supported by airpower drove deep into weak points in the Allied defence. Generally outfought by this *blitzkrieg*, the British and French carried out a withdrawal in contact towards the coast, and by early June the soldiers of the British Expeditionary Force had been evacuated by sea from Dunkirk, leaving all their heavy equipment behind on the beaches. The French were forced to surrender at an ignominious ceremony with Hitler and his generals on 22 June 1940.

Except for those troops of the subjugated countries who had also escaped from Europe and were determined to fight on for the liberation of their homelands, Britain now stood alone and faced the possibility of invasion for the first time since the Napoleonic wars. From June until September 1940, a huge works programme, largely coordinated by the Corps, was set in motion to provide fixed field defences all across England and Wales in preparation for the expected German invasion. At the same time, Corps units were involved in constructing highly secret operational bases across the whole country for the Auxiliary Units of the Home Guard.

As the majority of the shattered forces re-formed and re-equipped, the idea was initiated by Prime Minister Churchill that there should also be units capable of mounting amphibious raids to harry the German occupation forces on the mainland of Europe. Volunteers came from every part of the army, and the new units were called commandos because their function was to be similar to that of the Boer commandos during the South African War. A commando was about battalion size, but individuals continued to wear their

A Heavy Water Cell from Vermork.

parent cap badge. From 1942, a distinctive green beret was introduced – and this has since been copied by other armies as an indication of special duties forces. Many Sappers volunteered for commando service. Sergeant Thomas Durrant, RE, was awarded a posthumous Victoria Cross for his actions in the St Nazaire raid in 1942. German officers commended his gallantry. His award is understood to be the only Victoria Cross awarded to a soldier for a naval action at sea.

1940 also saw the raising of British airborne forces. On 22 June the Prime Minister issued an instruction that a corps of at least 5,000 parachute troops be raised. Some foreign armies had introduced parachutists in the early 1930s, and the German army had shown their effectiveness in the recent *blitzkrieg*. Despite having no previous relevant experience, Major J. F. Rock, RE, was appointed to take charge of the military organization of British airborne forces. As with the introduction of the commando units, arrangements were soon under way and the first brigade was in existence by 1941. Eventually there were to be two airborne divisions, the 1st and 6th, each comprising two parachute and one glider-borne brigade. The Royal Engineer elements were to be two parachute squadrons, a glider-borne field company and a glider-borne field park company.

The first Royal Engineer airborne units were 9 Field Company and 261 Field Park Company, both glider-borne; other units were raised later. Both units were involved in one of the first British airborne operations, Operation 'Freshman', which was mounted in November 1942 as a demolition attack on a heavy-water plant at Vermork in the Telemark district of southern Norway. Two gliders were towed 400 miles to the target by Halifax bombers, then the longest glider-tow ever attempted. Only one aircraft returned, and it was not until after the war that details of this operation were revealed. The German occupation forces executed all survivors of the landing

The Bomb Disposal Arm Badge.

force, and Norwegian saboteurs eventually completed the task. Apart from aircrew of the Royal Air Force, the Royal Australian Air Force and the Glider Pilot Regiment, the attack force was drawn entirely from the Royal Engineers. A memorial to them all now stands near Oslo.

In 1942 a maroon beret was adopted as the headdress for British airborne forces, and this has been copied by many other armies in a similar fashion to the green beret of commando forces.

In order to mount an amphibious invasion of Britain, the Germans first needed to gain air superiority. Although the expected seaborne invasion did not materialize, the preparatory attack from the air did, and what became known as the Battle of Britain ensued, bringing yet another new function for the Corps. Extensive air raids across the country raised the problem of unexploded bombs. The Royal Engineers were therefore given the responsibility of dealing with all enemy unexploded bombs, except on Royal Navy or Royal Air Force establishments, which those two services dealt with themselves. Working from little previous knowledge, some 400 Bomb Disposal Sections consisting of over 10,000 men had been formed by September 1940. They wore a special arm badge and painted the mudguards of their vehicles red for instant recognition. It was during these air raid activities that HM King George VI recognized the need for an award comparable to the Victoria Cross for equivalent gallantry, but not actually in the face of the enemy. The George Cross and the George Medal

Lieutenant (later Colonel) Stuart Archer, GC.

Greece. British and Empire troops were sent to help the Greeks but eventually had to be evacuated. The Germans were then able to reinforce the Italians in the North African desert after the latter had suffered several defeats at the hands of the British. The resulting desert campaign was to swing back and forth until October 1942 when, at the Battle of El Alamein, under the command of General Montgomery, the fortunes of war in the Middle East began to turn in favour of the Allies.

In 1941 the war really became a World War. In June, Germany invaded the Soviet Union, and in December, Japan launched a surprise onslaught on the United States Pacific Fleet at Pearl Harbor in the Hawaiian Islands, which brought America into the war. At the same time, British possessions in the Far East were invaded, and Hong Kong, Malaya and Singapore fell, followed by Burma in early 1942, the Japanese only being held on the very borders of India.

With the United States of America now in the war, there was agreement between the Allies that first priority would be given to defeating the Germans. The British Eighth Army thrust westwards in North Africa, pushing the Axis armies before it, and was joined in November 1942 by an Anglo-American force that had landed in Morocco and Algeria and was to push eastwards. By May 1943 the Germans surrendered, and the war in North Africa was over.

In the desert there was no call for bridging, and only a few bridges were needed in Morocco and Algeria. By far the most outstanding development for the Royal Engineers was mine warfare. Water supply was also high in importance, and much use was made of ancient Roman aquifers as well

were therefore instituted in 1940. By the time intensive bombing of Britain slackened off in 1943, 13 officers and men of the Bomb Disposal Service had been awarded the George Cross. Eventually bomb disposal units accompanied all expeditionary forces overseas.

North Africa, Sicily and Italy

With the fall of France in 1940, Italy declared war on Britain. This led to the commencement of operations in the Middle East. Italy invaded Egypt from Libya and was met by the pre-war British garrison reinforced by Empire troops from India, Australia, New Zealand and South Africa. Campaigns were also mounted to eject the Italians from Abyssinia and Eritrea, against former French allies in Syria, and against pro-German activists in Iraq. Meanwhile the Germans launched an offensive in the Balkans, overrunning Yugoslavia and as pipelines from Egypt. Road and airfield construction was aided by the gradual introduction into the Corps of various types of earth-moving machinery. The Americans had developed much of this equipment, and they also provided training in its use. One item of German equipment that was found to be superior to the Allied equivalent was the petrol container, the so-called 'jerrican', and it was decided to copy it. Until factory-made supplies could be obtained from Britain or America, a production line was set up in Royal Engineer workshops in Egypt. Local-pattern anti-tank mines were also made in quantity.

In the Mediterranean theatre of operations, there were two long-standing Royal Engineer stations. Between the outbreak of war and 1942, five Tunnelling Companies, one of them from the Royal Canadian Engineers, were employed in Gibraltar to cut more tunnels and provide further underground accommodation. The excavated rock was used to construct an airstrip projecting into the sea, which is still in use today. A Quarrying Company, Road Construction Company, Excavator Company, including a Canadian diamond-drilling section and Artisan Works Company were all involved in this work.

Malta suffered a siege and constant air attack from the time of Italy's entry into the war until the victory in North Africa in 1943. The resident 16th and 24th Companies were heavily involved in repairing damage and operating anti-aircraft and coast-defence searchlights (which had yet to be transferred to the Royal Artillery). 173 Tunnelling Company was also sent to the island to install important underground facilities, and two Bomb Disposal Sections were also kept fully employed. Until May 1942, the Governor of Malta was Lieutenant General Sir William Dobbie, a distinguished Royal Engineer officer. In April 1942, HM King George VI awarded the island the George Cross in recognition of the gallantry of the inhabitants and garrison.

Having rested and reorganized on the southern shores of the Mediterranean, the victorious Allied armies from North Africa invaded Sicily in July 1943 and crossed to the toe of Italy in September. That month Italy surrendered and joined the Allies, Mussolini having fallen from power in July. However, the Germans carried out a fighting withdrawal, making very effective use of Italy's mountains and rivers as defensive positions. To overcome an expert and determined enemy in such arduous conditions called for maximum effort in the skills of field engineering. Use of mechanical earth-moving equipment for road construction was commonplace, and armoured engineers made a first appearance.

Whereas mine warfare had been prominent in the desert campaign, bridging was to predominate in the Italian campaign, and the Bailey Bridge was forever to be linked with the Royal Engineers. Soon after the war started it became obvious that military bridging equipment needed to be upgraded to cater for constantly increasing military loads. Starting in December 1940, the staff of the Experimental Bridging Establishment and its chief designer Mr D. C. Bailey, later Sir Donald Bailey, produced a design for a new bridge within two months. By December 1941, a prototype had passed all tests, manufacture had begun, and the equipment was deployed to units. This versatile equipment bridge was simple, adaptable, and the components were easily transportable on standard vehicles. The American army also adopted it, and manufacture started in the United States. Pontoon bridges were also possible with Bailey equipment, and one of the first Bailey suspension bridges was built during the Italian campaign.

The need to train the Eighth Army Engineers and others in the new bridging equipment and other procedures developing in this new campaign led to the setting-up of engineer training facilities in Italy in early 1944. The Engineer Training Establishment was set up at Capua on the River Volturno consisting of a School of Military Engineering, a Polish School of Military Engineering, a Bridging Camp, an RE Training Depot, an Indian Engineers Training Depot and an Experimental Section, where

the Bailey Suspension Bridge was developed. Being very much an Allied army, engineers were British, American, Canadian, New Zealand, South African, Indian, French, Polish, Brazilian and Italian. The establishment also boasted its own opera house, at which the world-famous tenor Gigli performed,

Mention has been made that armoured engineers made an appearance in Italy. They were yet another new venture for the Corps, but to trace their beginnings we must go back to 1942. In August of that year the 1st Canadian Division made a large raid on the French coast at Dieppe. The intent was to test the challenges likely to be encountered by a major assault landing, leading to the capture of a port, and hard lessons were learnt at a very high

Nine Sapper Bridge.

cost in casualties. One item for the future was proposed by Lieutenant J. Donovan, Royal Canadian Engineers: an engineer tank, so that engineers could operate in the point of an armoured assault on prepared defences. The need for an engineer tank had been identified in 1919; a prototype was built, but no further progress was made at that time. Now its time had come, and the Churchill tank was selected because it was heavily armoured, had more room than other types and had side doors for easy loading and unloading. So the Assault Vehicle Royal Engineers came about. The tank gun was replaced with a petard device, which could project an 18-kg projectile designed to breach concrete walls about two metres thick. The engineer tank could also be adapted to carry an assault bridge or Bailey Bridge, bundles of brushwood (fascines) to fill anti-tank ditches, mine-ploughs, or a mine-flail to detonate anti-tank mines. Initially the drivers and radio operators were from the Royal Armoured Corps, but they were eventually rebadged as Royal Engineers. Trials and development proceeded urgently throughout 1943, and in due course the 1st Assault Brigade Royal Engineers was formed, largely from the personnel of Chemical Warfare Companies that had been disbanded. In parallel, 79th Armoured Division was formed to develop the armoured assault technique. The divisional commander was Major General

A Churchill AVRE.

Hobart, a Royal Engineer officer who had been prominent in the development of the tank after the Great War. In Italy during the winter of 1943/4, an Assault Regiment found from the Royal Engineers and the Royal Armoured Corps was formed with vehicles adapted in local workshops.

Normandy and North-West Europe

The fall of Rome to the Allies was over-shadowed by the opening of the Second Front in France – the invasion of Normandy on 6 June 1944. Ever since Dunkirk, the aim had been to return to the continent of Europe, and this now became possible, with the Germans overstretched by operations in Russia and by the full involvement of America in the war. Operation 'Overlord' was the largest and most comprehensive assault landing in history, and the ensuing campaign in North-West Europe was fought with an abundance of material and equipment never before equalled. Engineers had a major role to play, first to breach the coast defences and then to maintain the speed of

A General View of Mulberry 'B'.

advance. Not since the Crimean War had the Royal Engineers been so much in the forefront of the attack.

The main assault consisted of simultaneous amphibious landings on the Normandy coast by US, British and Canadian troops. Airborne landings on the night of 5/6 June protected the flanks – to the east by 6th Airborne Division. Their main tasks were to capture certain inland bridges, destroy or neutralize enemy coast-gun positions, and clear landing zones for gliders. The Royal Engineer units involved were 3 and 591 Parachute Squadrons, 249 Field and 286 Field Park Companies, the latter two units being inserted by glider. On the morning of 6 June 1944, the initial landing was by 8th Infantry Brigade which contained 246 Field Company, whose primary task was to clear a route forward for wheeled traffic. 77 and 79 Assault Squadrons, together with 629 Field Squadron and assisted by 263 Field Company, were to clear four zones each 200 metres wide through the beach obstacles and open eight exits from the beaches. Similar activities were taking place elsewhere on the British front by 50th Division

and 3rd Canadian Division. The worth of the Assault Engineers and their engineer tanks was soon proved.

The five specially trained Airfield Construction Groups RE also needed a rapid exit from the beaches. They also started landing on 6 June and next day completed the first emergency landing-ground for fighter-bomber aircraft. Within five days, six more airstrips had been prepared so that the RAF could maintain close support to the armies.

That some of these airstrips were in the general area of Bayeux is a reminder that the Bayeux Tapestry shows a portable fort brought over to England from Normandy by our direct antecedent, Humphrey de Tilleul. Now, in reverse, prefabricated artificial harbours, designed after an idea by Prime Minister Churchill but prompted by the lessons learned at Dieppe of the difficulty of capturing a port, were being moved from England to France. They were called Mulberry Harbours, and there were two, Mulberrry A being for the American beachhead and Mulberry B for the British. They had been designed and constructed, largely by Royal Engineer personnel, in great secrecy prior to the invasion and began moving over to France with the invasion fleet. Breakwaters were formed from old ships sunk in position, reinforced by prefabricated submersible concrete caissons. Connection to the shore was by floating piers and roadways. The Royal Engineer Port Construction Force was specially organized for the purpose, and parts of the harbour were ready to receive ships within nine days.

Unfortunately a four-day storm starting on 19 June destroyed the American Mulberry and badly damaged the British one. During their useful life, two and a half million men, half a million vehicles and four million tonnes of stores passed across the Mulberries. After ten months there was no longer any need for them because permanent ports had been recaptured and repaired for use. Remains of some of the concrete caissons can still be seen at Arromanches to this day.

Yet another innovation was Pipeline Under the Ocean, known by the acronym Pluto. This was a pipeline laid under the English Channel to carry fuel to the invading armies. Although not entirely a Royal Engineer project, the Corps was involved in laying over 700 kilometres of pipeline in Normandy and just over a further 1,100 kilometres into Germany.

After the breakout from the Normandy beachhead, Royal Engineer units were mainly involved in bridging, including the repair or replacement of bridges affected by enemy demolitions. A high proportion of new bridges were floating or pontoon bridges over the many rivers and canals. Just as important, to keep the logistics flowing, were roadworks. The very heavy traffic of the invading armies required repairs to existing roads and new bypasses around villages with narrow streets. A supply of clean and potable water – a division needed about 240,000 litres a day – necessitated the reinstatement of existing facilities as well as provision of water-points from rivers, streams and wells. Engineer operations also included mines. Extensive anti-tank and anti-personnel minefields were found inland, and these had to be cleared, while sometimes defensive minefields had to be laid. This pattern of engineer operations was repeated across northern France and Belgium until the entry into Holland in the autumn.

In September 1944, Operation 'Market Garden' was mounted. This was a great airborne assault to seize bridges over the Rivers Maas, Waal and Rhine, opening a corridor along which XXX Corps could punch its way into Germany, thus shortening the war. The operation was two-thirds successful in that the bridges over the Maas and Waal were seized by 82nd and 101st American Airborne Divisions. The British 1st Airborne Division was tasked to secure the Rhine bridges at Arnhem. Unfortunately, the area had been occupied by two German armoured divisions, which mounted immediate and heavy counterattacks on the airborne troops. The railway bridge was demolished by the enemy, but the road bridge was held by the 2nd Parachute Regiment against continued armoured attack. They were assisted by elements of 1 Parachute Squadron and 9 (Airborne) Field Company in close support. When their planned engineer tasks became no longer feasible, these Sappers fought with great gallantry as infantry under Captain E. M. Mackay, RE (who was to retire in 1977 as a major general and Chief Engineer, British Army of the Rhine). The lightly armed airborne troops fought against the German armour for ten days until the survivors were withdrawn across the Rhine in assault boats by 253 and 260 Field Companies of the 43rd Division, and by 20 and 23 Field Companies Royal Canadian Engineers in storm boats. Nearly 3,000 survivors were ferried to safety from 1st Airborne Division, which had started the operation 10,000 strong. Many were wounded and captured, and the airborne Sappers also suffered heavy casualties. Much has subsequently been written about the Battle of Arnhem, concentrating, quite naturally, on the paratroopers, but it should be remembered that the Royal Engineers played a very full part throughout, be they parachutist, glider-borne, or divisional troops.

Under cover of the harsh winter of 1944, and totally unexpectedly, the Germans launched a sudden and powerful counter-offensive against the Americans in the Ardennes. This thrust, which became known as 'the Battle of the Bulge', aimed to split the British and Canadians from the Americans and capture the main Allied supply seaport of Antwerp. It was the last throw of the dice for the Germans, and it required considerable Allied effort to blunt the attack and gradually push the enemy back.

Once the Ardennes operation was completed, the Allies began their main thrust into Germany to finish the war. This was to be a hard and brutal slog, for the Germans were now defending their home-land. The British thrust was aimed at the industrial Ruhr, and the last great obstacle was the River Rhine. 6th Airborne Division was again put in first to secure the east bank. To cross the river the assaulting infantry needed rafts, ferries and bridges, together with roads, approaches and exits at the crossing-points. Four floating bridges were built in the British sector, and five more were added later, while a similar bridging effort was also proceeding in the American sector. Booms also had to be constructed to protect the sites from damage by floating debris or enemy demolition squads. The Rhine crossings were an epic Sapper achievement and the result of meticulous planning. In 1943, units had practised crossing wide tidal rivers on the Great Yorkshire Ouse at Goole, and the necessary bridging equipment, boats, pontoons and outboard motors had been provided for just such a task as this.

With the Rhine crossed, the advance into Germany continued, with bridging still very much a main effort. One non-warfighting task was the need for four Royal Engineer Forestry Companies to produce pit-props to enable the Belgian coal mines to start production.

All German forces in North-West Germany surrendered to Field Marshal Montgomery's 21st Army Group on 4 May 1945, and the final instrument of surrender was signed at General Eisenhower's Allied Headquarters on 7 May 1945. The next day, 8 May, was officially named Victory in Europe, or VE, Day. All German forces in Italy had also surrendered on 2 May. The final months of the Italian campaign had been overshadowed by the events in North-West Europe, but to the end it was an arduous campaign and, for the Sappers, one in which bridge and road construction predominated.

The Far East

Attention now turned to the Far East, where operations continued by the British Fourteenth Army, consisting mainly of British, Indian and West African troops. But there were also other campaigns being waged by other British Commonwealth and US troops and the Chinese. In the summer of 1943 it was decided to coordinate the land and air forces of the British Commonwealth, the United States and the British Eastern Fleet under one command, called South East Asia Command, to take charge of all operations against the Japanese west of Singapore.

Earlier, we left the war in the Far East in 1942 with the Japanese on the borders of India. The main engineer tasks, as well as the defence of India, were now the construction of roads, railways and airfields ready for the reconquest of Burma. But, like the commando raids mounted on the coasts of Europe from the beleaguered UK, similar incursions were planned overland into Burma. The aim of this long-range penetration behind enemy lines was to harry the Japanese, disrupt their communications and gain experience for a future invasion. A brigade was specially trained and penetrated into Burma in small columns on foot. They were to become known as Chindits, and their activities under the most dreadful conditions have become legendary. Although no Royal Engineer units were in the force, several Royal Engineer officers and soldiers served as individuals. Prominent among these in the first force, which set out in early 1943, was Major J. M. Calvert, RE, known affectionately as 'Mad Mike', who commanded one of the columns. Despite constant Japanese attacks this column crossed several mountain

Crossing the Irrawaddy at Ngazun.

ranges, cut the railway in 75 places and destroyed two bridges. They were resupplied by air throughout, and by the time they returned no man had marched less than a thousand miles. This achievement lifted morale throughout Fourteenth Army because it proved that the Japanese soldier was no superman, and that our own troops, with suitable training, were more than equal to the Japanese in jungle fighting. But it must also be remembered that this jungle fighting was taking place in a country beset with mountain ranges, jungle, swamps, waterways and rivers, the latter being the main form of communication in the country. Burma is also dominated by the monsoon from May to October, and the very heavy rainfall makes a breeding ground for the mosquito. Malaria, dysentery, scrub typhus, and other tropical diseases were rampant.

In the spring of 1944 a second Chindit expedition was mounted by a much larger force of six brigade-sized columns, two of which were commanded by Royal Engineer officers, Brigadier L. E. C. M. Perowne and Mike Calvert, now appointed Brigadier. The aim of these columns was to establish firm bases in enemy-held country from which attacks on the Japanese could be mounted. This time, two of the brigades were flown in gliders, and Sappers with crawler tractors and other plant were included for airstrip construction so that the whole force could be sustained from the air. The chief British engineer units involved in this expedition were 2, 12, and 54 Field Companies and 219 Field Park Company.

At the same time, the Japanese were driven from the borders of India, and an offensive was launched towards the recapture of Mandalay. During this campaign, the longest operational floating Bailey Bridge in any theatre was built by Indian Engineers across the River Chindwin, at 351 metres long. In the spring of 1945 operations were also in hand on the coastal plain of Arakan to retake Rangoon. Landings were made by specially trained units, one of which included several Royal Engineers. Lieutenant C. Raymond, RE, second-in-command of one patrol, led a charge on an enemy post and won, posthumously, the second Royal Engineer Victoria Cross of the Second World War. The final assault on Rangoon was timed to take place on 2 May 1945, but the Japanese withdrew. By coincidence, Rangoon was reoccupied on the same day that the Germans surrendered in North-West Europe. A major amphibious operation was then planned for the recapture of Malaya, but before it could be mounted the United States dropped atomic bombs on the Japanese cities of Hiroshima and Nagasaki. On 14 August 1945 the Japanese surrendered unconditionally, and 15 August was officially named Victory over Japan, or VJ, Day.

Most of the engineer work in Burma was similar to that in the North African and Italian campaigns except that it was done in a tropical climate and a difficult environment. In no other campaign was air supply so prominent, so the Sappers had to develop the organization and techniques to produce dropping zones and airstrips very quickly. Improvisation and the use of local materials, coupled with the ability to apply the basic principles of engineering, were essential when equipment was not readily to hand. The Burma campaign was also the conclusion, as far as active service was concerned, of the great comradeship-in-arms that had existed between the British and Indian Armies for over two centuries.

And so, after six years, the Second World War came to an end. On 3 September 1939 the total Regular, Territorial and reservist strength of the Corps was nearly 60,000 all ranks. In 1945, in an army of three million, 281,000 (9.4 per cent) were Royal Engineers. When hostilities ceased, the Corps was spread across the world – as one of our mottoes says in Latin, Ubique, or 'Everywhere'. Wherever the Sappers were, safety catches were applied on weapons and tool-boxes opened, ready to make good the ravages of war.

POST-WAR WINDS OF CHANGE

An unusual commitment in the last stages of the war, continuing into 1946, was the requirement to train a new Netherlands army to operate in the Dutch East Indies, now Indonesia. This was an army commitment and in the Corps, English-speaking Dutchmen were included in Training Battalion Recruit Parties on the same footing as their British comrades. Later, some returned as Junior NCOs to help train non-English-speaking Dutchmen.

Meanwhile the field army was occupied chiefly in becoming an army of occupation in former enemy territory, or reoccupying British, Empire or Allied possessions abroad. In North-West Europe, the so-called British Liberation Army (21st Army Group) became the British Army of the Rhine (invariably referred to as BAOR). Germany was divided into four zones occupied by the forces of Britain, the USA, France and the Soviet Union. The British Zone was in the North-West part of Germany centred on Hannover. BAOR Engineers were thus conveniently sited to assist in the rehabilitation of Holland and Belgium. Within Germany, one of the prime tasks was to replace the many assault bridges over the River Rhine with semi-permanent Bailey Bridges. The city of Berlin was a special case; although in the Russian Zone it was itself divided into four sectors, each occupied by one of the Allied powers. The British Sector garrison was provided by the Berlin Infantry Brigade, which eventually was to have its own Engineer unit, 38 (Berlin) Field Squadron. In Austria, British Troops (Austria) were the British Occupation Forces for that country, having advanced from Italy when operations finished.

"From Stettin in the Baltic to Trieste in the Adriatic, an iron curtain has descended across the Continent."
– Churchill

In Japan, the British Commonwealth Occupation Force was under Australian command, 5 Field Company and 350 Field Park Company being part of it. Australian, New Zealand and Indian engineers were also included in the Force, which was the first completely integrated formation made up of units from various parts of the British Empire and Commonwealth. Similarly, Commonwealth engineer units assisted in the immediate post-war rehabilitation of the Dutch East Indies, French Indo-China and Thailand. The British possessions of Singapore, Malaya and Hong Kong were reoccupied in September 1945.

Regrettably 1945 did not see a return to total peace; indeed, various levels of active service were still required across the world. Internationally the greatest threats to peace were communist expansion spearheaded by our former wartime ally, the Soviet Union, and the advent of nuclear weapons. The period became known as the Cold War. However, the United Nations Organization came into being at this time with the hope that in future agreement rather than war could solve nations' differences.

An attempted communist take-over in Greece had started in 1944 when a large part of the German army was withdrawn. British troops were deployed until a truce was agreed at the end of 1945. As usual the Sappers were employed on general rehabilitation, particularly the building and repairing of bridges. Unrest restarted between Arabs and Jews in Palestine, aggravated by the influx of Jewish refugees from Europe wishing to establish a new state of Israel. Much of the insurgency was aimed at the British Mandate, so a considerable force of three divisions was progressively deployed to deal with the disorder. Engineer work involved constructing accommodation for these troops, searching for, and disposing of, mines and booby-traps, and operating in

General Service Medal with clasp Palestine 1945–48.

the infantry role. The fledgling United Nations was called in to negotiate a solution that was not entirely acceptable to all sides, and the British government gave up the mandate held since the end of the Great War, withdrawing in 1948.

The situation in Palestine became in some ways typical of events across the world in the ensuing years. Britain still had many responsibilities overseas despite the beginnings of a programme of independence for various Empire countries. Military garrisons were still required, but the wartime conscript soldiers were being demobilized because their conscription was for the duration of the war only. It was therefore decided in 1947 to retain conscription, to be called National Service, so that Britain could fulfil its responsibilities in the unstable post-war world. Initially men were conscripted for one year, extended in 1950 to two years with the Colours, followed by three-and-a-half years in the Territorial Army. Young men were allowed to complete apprenticeships or other professional training before doing their National Service, and thus for many years to come the Corps received some very well-qualified recruits and officer cadets – a lance corporal, RE, with a Bachelor of Science degree was not unusual! Although India and Palestine no longer required large numbers of British troops, garrisons had to be maintained in Egypt, Libya, Cyprus, Somaliland, Sudan,

Singapore, Malaya, Hong Kong, Gibraltar, Malta and the Caribbean in addition to the Armies of Occupation in Germany, Austria and Japan.

The Corps itself was not free from change over this period. In 1947, a regimental organization was adopted throughout the Corps. From experience during the war, it was considered that a regiment would be more efficient in support of a division than the previous semi-independent field companies organized as divisional engineers. By and large, the new regiments were composed of squadrons retaining their traditional numbers. There were other changes in nomenclature, the chief of which were that mechanical equipment became plant, the rank of Driver RE was abolished, and the trade of Field Engineer was introduced, later to be changed to Combat Engineer. In 1948 the Gurkha Engineers were raised.

In 1949 a new pattern of cap badge for the Corps was introduced to replace the bronze badge of the officers and the plain brass of the other ranks. Now the laurel wreath was to be in silver and the rest of the badge in gold for all ranks, and this pattern is still extant. After the Second World War many regiments and corps adopted more elaborate badges, so in this the Corps was not unique. At the same time the officers' collar badges were changed from bronze to gilt but were

changed back to bronze shortly afterwards. In 1950 a new ceremonial uniform for the army was announced. It was to be blue with a peaked cap, gold rank badges and traditional trouser stripes. A blue beret was included so that the uniform could be worn for 'walking-out', and the whole uniform was called No. 1 Dress. The intention was that it would be the parade uniform for the whole army, but for various reasons this never came about, although it was issued to troops for special occasions. No. 1 Dress is now used for military bands, certain ceremonial duties and senior officers' appointments. In 1951 the blue lanyard was introduced into the Corps to brighten up the battledress, again following the trend in other branches of the army. About the same time the blue beret from the No. 1 Dress became the universal headgear worn with battledress.

Getting back to peacetime soldiering, at least at home, did have some effect because

Marchwood Military Port.

57

the Corps began to head back to its traditional homes at Chatham and elsewhere in the south of England. On the outbreak of war in 1939 many training establishments had been moved away to avoid the expected enemy air raids and to provide a larger number of sites to cater for the increased size of the Corps. Locations were now to be:

School of Military Engineering. The Trade Training Wing for artisan training had remained at Chatham throughout the war to make use of the existing workshops. A much-enlarged Field Engineer School had been set up at Ripon, and this now moved to Gillingham, where it occupied the old Apprentice Training School accommodation at Fort Darland. The apprentices had moved out in 1940, after which Fort Darland had become a Detention Barracks. Fort Darland was now renamed Gordon Barracks.

Port Training Regiment. During the war, military ports had been specially built by the Corps at Faslane on Gare Loch and at Cairn Ryan near Stranraer in Scotland and later at Marchwood near Southampton, which was also used for Mulberry Harbour construction. Marchwood was now to become the establishment for Port and Inland Water Transport training.

Royal Engineer Depot. The Depot Battalion RE had originally moved to Halifax until the end of the war, when it moved to Barton Stacey, near Andover, and finally back to its original home at Kitchener Barracks, Chatham.

Railway Training Centre. This had remained at Longmoor throughout the war and now changed its title to Transportation Training Centre.

School of Military Survey. The Survey Training Centre had moved several times during the war and now settled under its new title at Hermitage, near Newbury, in Berkshire.

Mechanical Transport Training. The Royal Engineers Mounted Depot at Aldershot became the Mechanical Transport Depot on mechanization and had remained so all through the war, becoming 4 Training Regiment RE in 1947.

Field Training Regiments. Some ten Training Battalions RE for field engineer training had existed for varying periods during the war. With the retention of National Service, requiring intakes of trainees every two weeks, four regiments were still needed. These were located at Malvern (Worcestershire), Cove (near Aldershot), Elgin (Scotland) and Portland (Dorset). To control their activities and ensure uniform standards, Headquarters Training Battalions RE, under the command of a brigadier, was formed at Aldershot.

Although apprentices were enlisted to be the future technicians of the army, the War Office decided after the war to enlist boys for training as future non-commissioned officers. They were to be called Junior Leaders, and those for the Corps formed a squadron in 4 Training Regiment RE. In 1959 this was expanded to the Junior

Leaders Regiment RE and based in Dover.

From the rather parochial affairs of the Corps we must now return to the trouble-spots of the world. The continuing communist threat from Russia and her allies led to the formation of the North Atlantic Treaty Organization (NATO), with the USA taking a leading part in the defences of Europe. The Far East remained prominent, most of the troubles there stemming from the vacuum left after the wartime Japanese occupation, coupled with the spread of communism. The Malayan Emergency began in 1948 with a potential insurrection by the Chinese Communist Party. The anti-communist campaign was waged largely by a National Service army, although Commonwealth help was forthcoming from Australia, New Zealand, Rhodesia, Fiji, and units of the King's African Rifles. Malaya became independent in 1957 and Singapore in 1959, but the end of the Emergency was not finally declared until 1960. Throughout the years, the constant patrolling and hunting down of terrorists in the Malayan jungle was mainly an infantry task, but the Sappers played their vital part with the construction of helicopter landing sites and fire-support bases as well as the provision of water. Other engineer tasks were the traditional ones of barrack and camp building for the troops engaged in the campaign, as well as the construction of roads, airfields and bridges to open up the country. Map production was also vital because much of the area had to be resurveyed and existing maps updated. An Engineer Training Centre Far East was also formed to run courses similar to those at the School of Military Engineering at home. Air-trooping had not yet arrived, so units and individuals still moved across the world by troopship. The journey from the UK usually took three weeks to Singapore and Malaya and four to Hong Kong, so it was time-consuming to send men back to UK for relatively short courses. During this period the Gurkha Engineers and the locally enlisted Malayan Engineers were formed.

The Crown Colony of Hong Kong had barely been reoccupied after the Japanese withdrawal when, in 1949, the Communist People's Republic was proclaimed in China. Non-communist refugees poured into Hong Kong and, with the frontier threatened, the garrison was reinforced by 40th Division. The resident Royal Engineers were mostly Works Services units engaged on post-war rehabilitation work. They were now joined by the newly formed 24 Field Engineer Regiment comprising 11, 54 and 56 Field Squadrons and 15 Field Park Squadron. There followed a rapid programme of strengthening the border fence between the Hong Kong New Territories and Communist China, laying minefields and constructing defence posts. Meanwhile, the Works Services units were fully committed to building new camps to house the troops of 40th Division. Later two squadrons of the newly raised Gurkha Engineers were sent to the colony. One important part of the defences was the construction by the Corps of Route Twisk, an all-weather road along the mountainous spine of the New Territories. Owing to the lack of continuity in the supply of manpower because of constant turnover of National Servicemen, the Hong Kong Squadron Royal Engineers was formed comprising Field, Works, Bomb Disposal

Water Point at Pintail Ridge, Korea.

and Plant Troops manned with locally enlisted Chinese Sappers. This resident unit was later redesignated 82 Independent Hong Kong Squadron RE.

Unrest in the Far East next surfaced in Korea, which had also been occupied by Japan during the Second World War. After the war, Korea had been split into the communist North and the free South. In June 1950 the North Korean army, well-equipped by Russia and China, invaded South Korea. American troops were sent from Japan to assist with protecting the sovereignty of South Korea, and the United Nations called on other countries for support. Initially, British troops were sent from Hong Kong, but later 29th Infantry Brigade, which included 55 Field Squadron RE, provided reinforcement from the UK. At first the United Nations forces were successful and drove the North Koreans back, only stopping on the Yalu River, the border with China. China then intervened to support North Korea, and the war eventually stagnated into one of trench warfare similar to

the Great War of 1914–18. Engineer work included all aspects of field or combat engineering but was aggravated by the harsh Korean climate. This ranged from tropical heat in the summer to Arctic cold in the winter; indeed, the normal tour of duty in the campaign for units or individuals was reckoned to be 'one winter'. The United Nations forces were under American command, and the British Commonwealth forces were amalgamated to form the 1st Commonwealth Division, the engineer element comprising 28 (Commonwealth) Field Engineer Regiment of British, Canadian and New Zealand Sappers; 12 and 55 Field Squadrons and 64 Field Park Squadrons were the main British components. Another Commonwealth Engineer Regiment existed at the United Nations base in Japan called BRITCOM Engineer Regiment and was based on a unit of the Royal Australian Engineers that had been part of the Occupation Forces. A truce was finally agreed between the belligerents in July 1953, and the Armistice then agreed is still in force. One outcome of the Korean War and its harsh climate was recognition of the shortfalls in personnel equipment, much of which was a legacy from the Second World War. This led to the development and issue of combat dress, parkas, sleeping bags, and boots with directly moulded soles, which are common today. This uniform was originally olive-green; gradual developments and change in style led to the present disruptive-pattern material, adopted in 1971.

With the Malayan Emergency and the Korean War at their height, trouble erupted in Africa in 1952. In Kenya, the Kikuyu tribe founded a secret and sinister organization called the Mau-Mau and began a murderous campaign against both Europeans and Africans from other tribes. Lessons learned in Malaya were invaluable in defeating this insurrection, and engineer tasks were mainly laying roads and tracks to aid the deployment of security forces. 39 Corps Engineer Regiment, comprising 72 and 73 Field Squadrons and 74 Field Park Squadron, constructed 380 kilometres of road in the Aberdare Forest and 650 kilometres in the Mount Kenya forest regions. In 1955 the regiment provided hutted communal buildings and hot-water installations in British camps before returning to the UK to disband, leaving 73 Squadron as a composite independent squadron. Survey also played a big part in this campaign, as the local maps were not good enough for the Security Forces, so 89 Field Survey Squadron was formed specifically

Africa General Service Medal with clasp Kenya.

for the task. The Mau-Mau rebellion was largely defeated by 1956, and the squadron was disbanded three years later.

Cyprus was the next trouble-spot. In 1954, a secret organization called EOKA, led by a Greek general called Grivas, and in favour of the union of Cyprus with Greece, began the familiar terrorist pattern of riots, sabotage, assassination and guerrilla attacks. This was just at the time when the UK was in the process of moving its Middle East Command from Egypt, where there had also been civil disorder. Corps involvement in Cyprus was already high, with Works Services personnel and 35 Army Engineer Regiment engaged in providing the facilities for the new Middle East Command. 35 Regiment became increasingly involved in internal security duties, and further troops, including 37 Corps Engineer Regiment, were deployed to deal with the insurgency. 42 Survey Engineer Regiment also moved to Cyprus as part of Headquarters Middle East Land Forces. EOKA violence ceased in 1958 and Cyprus became independent in 1960 with the exception of about 300 square kilometres called the Sovereign Base Areas. These bases, in the east at Dhekelia and in the west at Episkopi and Akrotiri, remain vital as forward mounting bases for operations in the Middle East.

In July 1952 King Farouk of Egypt was deposed; two years later Gamal Abdul Nasser became president, and in 1956 he nationalized the Suez Canal Company.

Britain and France were major shareholders in the company, and both saw continued universal access to the canal as a vital national interest; in November an Anglo-French force intervened. The British element was II British Corps. The initial airborne assault included 9 Independent Parachute Squadron RE, and other participating Royal Engineer units included 36 and 38 Corps Engineer Regiments, while 35 Engineer Regiment was given a port-operating role along with 8 Railway Squadron RE and 51 Port Squadron RE. Reservists were recalled to the Colours to bring units to war establishment, and specialist units of the Army Emergency Reserve were mobilized. 42 Survey Regiment in Cyprus was also fully committed to map production. Cyprus itself was used as a base for the

Megaton test, Christmas Island.

preparation and launching of the attack on Port Said. In the event, the initial success of the air and sea landings and the defeat of the Egyptian forces was overtaken by political censure led by the United States, and the force was withdrawn in December, to be replaced by a United Nations force of Norwegians, Danes, Swedes, Colombians, Indians and Yugoslavs.

The atomic bombs dropped by the United States on Japan to end the Second World War had been developed under American management by a team of scientists from a variety of countries. When the team was broken up and the United States

government restricted further development to its own scientists, the British government set up its own organization called the Atomic Weapons Research Establishment. Kiloton and megaton devices were developed, and the Corps provided the bulk of the infrastructure support to test them. The first test in the kiloton range was held in 1952 as an ocean surface-burst off the Monte Bellos Islands near Australia, with further firings in 1956. These were followed by tests of the effects on military equipment at the Maralinga Proving Grounds in South Australia during 1956–7. Tests of megaton devices were held on Christmas Island in the Pacific, 2° north of the Equator, and some 1,900 kilometres from Honolulu in the Hawaiian Islands, over the period 1956 to 1959. The island is the largest coral atoll in the world, some 56 kilometres long and 27 kilometres wide. As some of these devices were to be air-dropped, the RAF provided the Task Force Commander. As well as assisting with the actual tests, the Corps had to build up the base almost from scratch by constructing living accommodation in prefabricated hutting, roads, port facilities and water and power supplies. A wartime airfield also had to be refurbished and a second built. The following units each spent about a year on Christmas Island in support of the series of tests, forming part of Task Force Grapple:

28 Field Engineer Regiment (fresh from Korea as part of the Commonwealth Engineer Regiment)
25 Field Engineer Regiment
38 Corps Engineer Regiment
36 Corps Engineer Regiment
12 Independent Field Squadron also spent 1958–9 on the island and a troop of 51 Port Squadron was part of the Task Force throughout, together with 504 Postal Unit
73 (Christmas Island) Squadron was formed in 1957 as a base unit to take over and maintain all the new buildings and facilities as they were built
Two troops of the Fiji Military Forces, some of whom were Sappers, also took part from February 1958.

By International Agreement, a moratorium on nuclear testing in the atmosphere came into effect at the end of 1958, so no more tests were done from 1959. Construction of the Christmas Island base was completed in that year, after which 17 Independent Field Squadron, having been specially trained, arrived to mothball all the facilities. The base was reopened and used again briefly in the early 1960s in support of the American space programme.

From the earliest times the Corps had been responsible for the army's buildings, but in 1959 a government committee decided that Works Services for the army should be taken over by a civilian War Department Works Organization. This would relieve the Corps from being responsible for providing the multifarious buildings and services required in peacetime by the army. The decision was reinforced by the fact that a large programme of rebuilding was about to be put in hand to modernize or rebuild most of the military estate, and therefore, given manpower constraints, a much larger organization was required than Royal Engineers Works Services could provide. In fact, the worldwide transfer of responsibilities took well into the 1960s, and the War Department Works Organization was subsequently absorbed into the newly founded Ministry of Public Building and Works. This organization was retitled the Property Services Agency in 1963 and was made responsible for all government building, including that for the three armed services. Nevertheless, Royal Engineer personnel remained responsible for Works Services in operational areas, and individual officers and technicians were allotted posts within the civilianized works organizations in order to maintain expertise.

THE END OF NATIONAL SERVICE AND MORE SMALL WARS

Peacetime conscription ended with the call-up of the last National Servicemen during 1960 – from 1 January 1963 the Regular army was once again to be an all-volunteer force. The early 1960s also saw the introduction into the Corps of the 7.62mm Self-Loading Rifle (to suit NATO standardization) as the soldier's personal weapon. The rifle was a British adaptation of a Belgian design and replaced bolt-action rifles that, in various forms, had been in service for some eighty years. The BREN light machine-gun was also re-chambered to take the new ammunition, and a new, heavier, belt-fed general-purpose machine-gun, also 7.62mm, was introduced to replace the Vickers medium machine-gun.

In 1962 issue began of a new No. 2 Dress for other ranks to replace the wartime serge battledress. For the first time barathea material, similar to that used in officers' uniforms, was used. A modern derivative of this uniform remains in use today and is the Parade Dress for the army.

In 1961 the close connection between the Corps and the Royal Navy and Royal Marines in Chatham came to an end with the rundown of the dockyard and the RN barracks, HMS *Pembroke*. In 1962, the School of Military Engineering celebrated its 150th anniversary since being formed by Major Pasley in 1812. As a birthday present, Her Majesty the Queen bestowed the Royal title on the school, henceforward to be known as the Royal School of Military Engineering. This was announced by His Royal Highness the Duke of Edinburgh, who was visiting Chatham to lay the foundation stone of a new barracks at Chattenden. When Chattenden Barracks was complete, Gordon Barracks in Gillingham was demolished.

Various units of the Corps inevitably became involved when British Honduras (now Belize) was struck by Hurricane 'Hattie' in 1961. 12 Field Squadron of 38 Corps Engineer Regiment was flown in at short notice to assist with relief work and reconstruction; 20 Field Squadron, who rebuilt Airfield Camp, followed them in 1962. Flood relief in Kenya was the lot of 25 Field Squadron of 36 Corps Engineer Regiment in 1962. The Corps also dealt with other small disasters in the Cameroons, Kuwait and Bahrain. In 1963, Skopje in Yugoslavia suffered an earthquake; international aid (which included Russian troops) included the deployment of 35 Corps Engineer Regiment from the British Army of the Rhine, which built 244 Nissen Huts as temporary accommodation.

Throughout the 1960s small wars continued around the world, and the Corps continued to play its key part in helping the army to fight, move and live. Trouble in the Middle East and Far East rumbled through the decade. At the end of 1962, internal security operations in Sarawak and Brunei, on the island of Borneo, called for airfield maintenance, construction of forward airstrips and the maintenance of public utilities. This was done mostly by Gurkha and Malayan Engineers led by their British officers and SNCOs. In 1963, Indonesian terri-

"Roll on death, de-mob's too far away." – Anon

64

torial aspirations against Sarawak led to the Borneo Confrontation. The British garrison was therefore increased, and camp facilities were needed to house them. Four field squadrons, one of which was Australian, were employed on jungle base, road, bridge, airstrip and helipad construction as well as on the major task of providing purified water. The Australian squadron built a total of 182 kilometres of road. This campaign, in savage jungle terrain, lasted until 1966.

The Middle East troublespots were Aden and Cyprus. Ethnic tensions had existed in Cyprus between the Greek and Turkish populations since independence in 1960. They came to a head towards the end of 1963, and the British garrison was mobilized as a peacekeeping force to keep the two sides apart. The two resident Royal Engineer units, 33 Field Squadron and the Cyprus Park Squadron, were turned out on Christmas Night 1963, 33 Field Squadron soon moving to Nicosia, the capital, to act as infantry as well as carrying out their normal Sapper tasks. A dividing line between the two sides was soon established, the so-called 'Green Line', a term since used elsewhere in similar circumstances. (It became known as this because it was drawn on the map by the Commander Royal Engineers, Lieutenant Colonel M. Andrews, OBE, RE, in green pencil!) Additional troops were also sent from the UK, including 16th Parachute Brigade and 9 Parachute Squadron RE. By March 1964 a United Nations Peacekeeping

United Nations Medal, Cyprus.

Force was installed consisting of British, Canadian, Danish, Swedish, Finnish and Republic of Ireland troops plus Australian civil police. The normal British garrison returned to its Sovereign Base Areas but remained in support of the UN Force, which is still in place today (2006), despite a subsequent invasion of northern Cyprus by Turkish forces in 1974. Early in 1964 Cyprus Park Squadron (assisted by 33 Field Squadron) constructed a 914-metre airstrip for the RAF at the Dhekelia base in three weeks, to improve flexibility of communications.

Trouble in Aden had been brewing since tribal unrest in 1955–8, but the South Arabian Peninsula was well-known for continuing tribal feuds. Britain had promised independence to South Arabia in 1968, with a centre of government in Aden, and to this end various facilities were built up between 1962 and 1964. These were not only to house an enlarged British garrison until 1968 but to hand over to the new independent government and its emerging Regular army. Royal Engineer Works Services personnel were heavily involved in this project, assisted by 32 Field Squadron, who were responsible for track and camp construction. However, two rival nationalist groups, supported by Egypt and Yemen, began to jockey for power with a campaign of terrorism, which led to the Radfan campaign of 1964. To support this campaign, the Dhala Road was built to improve access in this barren and mountainous country. The road ran from Aden to

Dhala, which was nearly 2,000 metres above sea level in the north and near the border with Yemen. Between 1964 and 1966 approximately 64 kilometres of road was built partly on the site of an earlier road by 3, 9 Parachute, 20, 24, 30, 48, 50 and 73 Field Squadrons and 6 and 63 Field Park Squadrons. 131 Parachute Engineer Regiment from the Territorial Army also played a part in the construction. This large number of units was necessary because six months was about as long as a squadron could spend on the project without relief – not only because of the inhospitable terrain and climate (at midday it was possible to fry an egg on the bonnet of a Land Rover) but also because of the frequent attacks by dissidents. Plant operators carried their personal weapons at all times, and working parties were protected by Royal Engineer picquets. It was also decided to blacktop the road to hinder the dissident practice of burying mines in the surface. What had

started as a nine-month project for a field park squadron had taken 31 months to complete, giving all ranks experience as soldiers, Sappers and tradesmen in very trying operational conditions. The British government finally evacuated the garrison, which had been in-country for 128 years, at the end of 1967, after a most frustrating campaign. Coupled with the Borneo Confrontation, this was the spur to the government decision to withdraw from 'east of Suez' and to concentrate on Britain's commitment to Europe as part of the North Atlantic Treaty Organization.

In 1962, 42 Field Survey Regiment returned to the UK from Cyprus after service abroad since 1940. The regiment and its predecessors had surveyed and produced maps of nearly three-quarters of a million square kilometres in Iraq, Kuwait, Oman, Aden, Jordan, Cyprus and Kenya. In the same year, the Royal Engineers Postal Service became tri-service, handling mail

Habilayn Airfield, Radfan.

Crown Airfield, Thailand.

for the RN and RAF and eventually changing its title to the Postal and Courier Communications Service. 1962 also saw the end of sea trooping, and the succession of troopships that over the years had carried British servicemen and their families to their overseas stations. The Corps had been much involved in this with the Embarkation Staffs of the Movement Control service, but in future trooping was to be by air using the Royal Air Force or civil airline contract. In March 1962 another connection with the history of the Corps disappeared with the demolition of the old balloon shed at Gibraltar Barracks, Aldershot. This had existed since the earliest days of military flying and the later Air Battalion RE. The barracks itself was also later demolished as part of the rebuilding (throughout the 1960s) of what was called Aldershot Military Town. The Corps had been responsible for

the design and building of all the original barracks in Aldershot that were now to be replaced or modernized.

One other task that came to the Corps was the construction of an airfield in Thailand. This was politically driven as part of the overall effort to blunting the spread of communism in the Far East and was carried out by existing units in the Far East rather than the new specialist airfield squadrons. Operation 'Crown' got under way in 1964 for the construction of an airfield and hutted camp by 11 and 59 Field Squadrons, a detachment of the RAF airfield construction branch and Australian and New Zealand Sappers. It was opened in 1965, but, following a very wet monsoon season, the runway had to be strengthened in 1966 to make it all-weather capable, 34 Field Squadron coming from the UK to assist. Operation 'Post-Crown' then started to build a road system to link inhabited areas in an underdeveloped part of Thailand much aggravated by communist subversion. Forty kilometres had been built by early 1968 when the troops were withdrawn, 54 Field Support Squadron from Singapore being the final unit involved

On 1 April 1964 the War Office itself disappeared, amalgamating with the Admiralty and Air Ministry to became the Ministry of Defence, the Chief of the Imperial General Staff becoming simply Chief of the General Staff. The biggest change for the Corps was announced in 1965 as the result of the findings of the government's McLeod Committee. This recommended a rationalization of functions within the armed services, particularly the formation of a Royal Corps of Transport. Hitherto, the Royal Army Service Corps carried out a dual function of supply, mostly rations and barrack stores, and transport. Now, the responsibility for all stores supply, except for Royal Engineer matériel, would be transferred to the Royal Army Ordnance Corps, and all land and sea transport would be the responsibility of the new Corps. This meant that the whole Transportation Branch of our Corps, comprising docks, ports, railways, and the Movement Control Service, was transferred on 15 July 1965, construction, maintenance, and repair of ports and railways remaining a Royal Engineer responsibility. 1,300 Sappers of all ranks were rebadged into the Royal Corps of Transport, and just over 200 transferred to the Royal Electrical and Mechanical Engineers.

The loss of these posts from the Corps was partially offset by another decision that the Airfield Construction Branch of the RAF should become a Royal Engineer responsibility. Some RAF personnel transferred into the Corps, but the raising of the Field Squadrons (Airfields) took place gradually at Waterbeach, near Cambridge. Initially, 10 and 60 Squadrons were made into airfield squadrons specifically for the Middle East, but they subsequently reverted to normal field squadrons. 51 Field Squadron (Airfields) was raised in the Far East but joined what had become 39 Engineer Regiment (Airfields) at Waterbeach in 1968. More recently, the airfields squadrons were retitled Field Squadrons (Construction), which is probably more appropriate because employment in such a unit usually meant concentration on a Sapper's artisan trade. At the time of writing, all Royal Engineer units in support of the RAF now have the suffix Air Support.

While these changes and new responsibilities for the Corps were in hand, a small return to our roots took place. In 1965 the last tunnel in Gibraltar was started, and when it was completed in 1968 the Tunnelling Troop was disbanded, 186 years after Sergeant-Major Ince had started it all.

There were other changes afoot during this period. In 1964–5, the Germany-based field squadrons became armoured in the sense that they were re-equipped with FV 432 armoured personnel carriers like the infantry, 1st Field Squadron RE being the first to be so re-equipped. In 1965, as a result of experience in Borneo and Southern Arabia, it was decided to form Specialist Teams Royal Engineers, which could plan and manage works projects worldwide. Specialist Teams were also established for certain specialist works in the Survey Branch. In 1967 the Medium Girder Bridge came into service and over the period 1967–8, Park Squadrons were retitled Support Squadrons. In 1966 the new Chattenden Barracks for the Royal School of Military Engineering was opened and, in 1967, 33 Field Squadron returned to the UK having been one of the resident Royal Engineer units in Cyprus. In 1968, 53 Field Squadron (Construction) started a 14-month project in the Caribbean building an airfield for the government of the British Virgin Islands to exploit tourism. The following year, 52 Field Squadron (Construction) deployed to RAF El Adem in Libya to extend the existing concrete runways.

But the decade closed on a grim note. In 1969, sectarian violence broke out in the city of Londonderry in Northern Ireland after a Civil Rights march. Once again the army was committed to internal security operations, only this time much closer to home. 3 Field Squadron was the first Sapper unit deployed to the province and was tasked with building accommodation in security-force bases and constructing a Peace Line in Belfast to keep the Loyalists and Nationalists apart. It was to mark the beginning of a bloody involvement lasting more than thirty years.

NORTHERN IRELAND

The army deployed to support the civil power in the province of Northern Ireland in 1969. Republican terrorism in both parts of the island of Ireland is not new, but the campaign precipitated in 1969 was perhaps the most costly in terms of lives and in investment of military capability. From 1969 to 1971 the ultra-militant Provisional Irish Republican Army grew in strength and in Republican areas such as West Belfast, North Londonderry and South Armagh the police, supported by the army, had regular contacts in their campaign to maintain the operational initiative. After Operation 'Motorman' in 1971 to support the internment of terrorist suspects, in which engineer tanks from 26 Armoured Engineer Squadron were deployed from Höhne in Germany, the Sapper involvement of a Field Squadron

"If any year in Northern Ireland deserved to be called the year of the Sapper it was 1986. By the end of last year the Sappers had completely re-built two Police stations and increased protection at thirty other Police stations and Army bases. In addition the Royal Engineers themselves designed new forms of blast walls, a new design of protected accommodation for Police stations and a new type of roof to overcome the effects of a mortar bomb. In the past year there is no doubt that lives have been saved and injuries prevented as a direct result of the additional protection provided by the Royal Engineers." – Sir John Stanley, the Minister for the Armed Forces, 1987

based in Antrim with a troop detached at Shackleton Barracks near Londonderry was increased. Field Squadrons now supported the three operational brigades, 3rd Brigade in Armagh, 8th Brigade in Londonderry and 39th Brigade in Belfast,

Barricade Removal in the Bogside.

all under the command of a lieutenant colonel and a small staff based in Lisburn at Headquarters Northern Ireland. 33 Independent Field Squadron, permanently stationed at Antrim from 1974, supported 39th Infantry Brigade with 325 Engineer Park, also at Antrim, providing engineer logistic support to the whole province. United Kingdom Land Forces and BAOR provided the other two squadrons on four-month tours. They were located at Castledillon and Ballykelly. Such tours provided a welcome change from the training routine and an opportunity for operational experience and team-building. Engineer regiments were also deployed in an infantry role.

By 1980 the various factions involved in the troubles had settled down to a near-

stalemate, with steady attrition of the terrorists by the security forces accompanied by sporadic outbursts of paramilitary violence. The start of the decade also saw a change in the tactics used by the army to support the overall security policy. The General Officer Commanding wished to establish the army firmly in a supporting role to the police. The emphasis was placed on covert rather than overt operations, and commanders were directed to consider reducing force levels where it was militarily possible. In June, 2 Armoured Division Engineer Regiment left Fort Monagh, the last major Royal Engineer unit to be deployed to Northern Ireland in an infantry role.

The new decade also started with an encouraging reduction in terrorist activity, and 1980 proved to be the least violent year for a decade. However, any optimism was short-lived, as a new threat to peace and stability emerged. For two years a number of Republican prisoners in the Maze Prison had been taking part in a so-called 'dirty' protest, and in October 1980 this escalated into a full hunger-strike. This were called off in December, but a further campaign of hunger-strikes began in 1981, resulting in the deaths of ten strikers and causing unprecedented reaction from Republicans. The upsurge in violence saw the return of street barricades, and 33 Field Squadron were fully committed. In two months the squadron plant teams moved over a thousand vehicles, while two of the field troops were deployed in the infantry role to relieve hard-pressed infanteers.

During every IRA campaign, South Armagh has been the focus of support for the terrorists. Its hilly and wooded countryside is difficult territory for military operations and has, quite correctly, been given the name 'bandit country'. The terrain is ideal for terrorist ambush, making movement by vehicle dangerous and helicopter the transport of choice. The Corps had been undertaking defensive works in the region since 1971.

In the late 1970s it was clear that more sophisticated protection was required, and the first major project using the new standards was at the police station at Crossmaglen, which was very cramped and highly vulnerable to mortar attacks. The Corps completed the project, called Operation 'Babel', between 1979 and 1981. The next base to receive attention was at Forkhill. Here the GOC demanded a more rapid and economic plan to protect both police and

army. This was rebuilt during Operation 'Consult' and completed in 1982. At Crossmaglen, following the completion of the new police building, the old police station was demolished by the Sappers to allow the construction of a new army base on the vacant site. Work started in 1980, and the building was handed over in February 1982. The four years of construction work in South Armagh provided first-class experience of operational project work. The logistic challenges were enormous. Only men and minor items of equipment could travel by helicopter. All major items, such as bulk materials, pre-cast concrete panels, structural steelwork and construction plant, had to be transported by road and stored in the already overcrowded bases until needed. A resupply operation usually took between three and four days and required two infantry battalions, ten specialist RE search teams and up to forty vehicles. Such operations were mounted every two or three months when between 400 and 1,000 tonnes of materials and equipment were moved to site. The need to forward plan and coordinate the very fine detail was paramount.

Following the completion of the South Armagh projects, there was a re-allocation of brigade responsibilities resulting in the disbanding of 3rd Infantry Brigade. The roulement thus reduced from a squadron to a troop in August 1982. 32 Field Squadron, as the last full squadron, had a very busy tour closing down the Castledillon base while finishing off the South Armagh projects. During this period the Royal Ulster Constabulary took over more control of security force operations, and yet the Sapper workload never seemed to reduce – perhaps because there were less Sappers to employ, there being only the resident 33 Field Squadron supported by the roulement troop. The bomb that destroyed Andersontown police station involved 33 Field Squadron for a number of weeks and also provided the opportunity to extend and improve the base. The erection of new sangars throughout the province was a constant commitment as units came and went, tactics changed and designs improved. Search teams were also kept busy, not only in undertaking the many duties required of the teams but also in providing the training of all-arms teams and in improving and trialling new procedures and equipment. Border crossings were high on the list of constant irritations and many efforts were made to keep them closed either by demolition or by placing obstacles to deter traffic.

The overall level of terrorist violence in 1985 fell to the lowest level for fifteen years, and in November that year a major political milestone was reached with the signing of the Anglo-Irish Agreement, which, for the first time, gave the Irish government a significant say in the affairs of Northern Ireland. There was deep-seated opposition to this agreement, resulting in an upsurge in sectarian attacks by Loyalists. At the same time the Provisional Irish Republican Army mounted a concentrated campaign against the police and their families, with hundreds of attacks on police houses and frequent mortar attacks on police stations. In 1987 the Remembrance Day massacre at Enniskillen marked a particularly horrific milestone. The IRA intended 1988 to be a year of escalating violence, and only strenuous efforts by the security forces prevented

much worse. The engineer activity during this period was dominated by the need to counter attacks on security-force bases involving the use of home-made mortars, projected grenades and improvised explosive devices. Thwarted by the creation of mortar-proof bases in South Armagh, the terrorists launched attacks on other softer bases across the province. Many of the army bases were made up of clusters of temporary buildings and were therefore very vulnerable to mortar attack. To counter this growing threat the Commander Land Forces tasked the Corps with a feasibility study into the provision of mortar protection to soft-skinned buildings. An initial reconnaissance of all 85 army bases in the province was completed in a week and 35 recommended for protective measures. The subsequent construction of blast-walls round the buildings in these bases was known as Operation 'Niccola' and ran from August 1985 to June 1986. Initially, the resident sub-unit, 33 Field Squadron, was deployed on the task, but the scale of the operation required reinforcement for a four-month emergency tour by 20 Field Squadron. A total of over 2,000 metres of high-density blockwork and the same amount of reinforced concrete-slab wall were constructed. 20 Field Squadron finished their tour in February 1986, and 33 Field Squadron completed Operation 'Niccola' by the end of May that year.

In late 1985, a campaign of attacks against police bases was commenced, mainly using home-made mortars. Plans to rebuild stations were hurriedly drawn up by the police authority for Northern Ireland, and the work was contracted to civilian firms – but before any major work could commence the terrorists began to intimidate the firms, causing them to withdraw from their contracts. The army was asked to help, and 20 Field Squadron took on the rebuilding of the police station at Ballygawley. From first tasking to handover, the project took eight weeks and was completed satisfactorily two days before 20 Field Squadron left the province. 42 Field Squadron arrived from Germany in February 1986 and worked exclusively for the next four months on Operation 'Jole 2' repairing damaged police stations at Toomebridge, Coalisland, Belcoo, Enniskillen and Bessbrook. 33 Field Squadron meanwhile repaired Carrickmore police station. The repair of the police station at Coalisland included the installation of a mortar-proof roof, a design developed in-house. Between July and November 1986, 30 Field Squadron erected 21 mortar-proof roofs at army bases across the province.

The 1991–2 armed services reorganization known as 'Options for Change' had implications for the Sappers in the province. The continuing roulement requirement imposed a heavy burden on the Corps, and the case was successfully argued for a resident engineer regiment in the province, to be based in a new base at Antrim and consisting of RHQ 25 Engineer Regiment with 12 Field Squadron and 43 Field Support Squadron. 25 Regiment would also take under command the existing resident units, 33 Independent Field Squadron and 325 Engineer Park. By August 1993 the new regiment was firmly established, but manpower pressures prevented full implementation and the decision was taken to disband 12 Field Squadron and transfer the

Sappers manning a mini-crowd control barrier during training for Northern Ireland.

number to the Headquarters Squadron of 25 Regiment. Therefore, for the foreseeable future, 25 Regiment would continue to have a roulement Field Squadron. By September 1997 the reorganization was completed with the regiment based in the newly built Massereene Barracks in Antrim.

The closing months of 1993 were dominated by the prospect of an end to the terrorist campaign brokered, in the main, by the then President of the United States, Bill Clinton. But, amid all the talk and speculation about peace, it was the actuality of violence on the streets that still preoccupied the police and army. Finally in December 1993 the Downing Street Declaration paved the way, in 1995, for a declaration of a cease-fire by Republican and Loyalist terrorists. All forms of violence were reduced except for punishment assaults. To date, this ceasefire has largely held, and there is hope, with both the Provisionals and certain Loyalist groups having repudiated violence and destroyed their weapons in the latter part of 2005, that the future of Ulster can be decided peacefully via the ballot box.

The political process towards peace has required the security forces to respond in kind. The police and Home Service battalions of the Royal Irish Regiment have been reorganized, and a process called Northern Ireland Normalization has begun. This will see the army elements of the security forces replaced with a conventional garrison (probably to be found from 19 Light Brigade), as in other parts of the United Kingdom. For the Corps this will involve the return of 25 Engineer Regiment to the mainland to re-role as an Air Support Regiment and its probable replacement by 38 Engineer Regiment, 19 Brigade's close-support engineers.

CHANGES CONTINUE BUT VARIETY REMAINS

The year 1971 saw the formal withdrawal of British forces from Singapore as part of the continuing process of independence for British colonies and territories. The Australia, New Zealand and United Kingdom Force was created as part of a five-power agreement with Malaysia and Singapore in order to retain a military presence in the area and to forestall external threats. Within 28 ANZUK Brigade there was a field squadron, based on 9 Field Squadron Royal Australian Engineers, which contained a British element of a field troop and certain posts within the squadron headquarters and support troop. This had been found from 37 Engineer Regiment at Longmoor. In time, the squadron became totally integrated, its main task being the close support of the three national battalions in 28th ANZUK Brigade by means of bridge and road construction, water supply and the building of jungle fire-support bases.

The British government's political intent was to achieve a reduction of overseas garrisons in order to concentrate British military power in Europe as part of the North Atlantic Treaty Organization alliance, where the threat from Russia and her allies in the Warsaw Pact was becoming greater. However, parts of the Middle East remained on the boil. In the Persian Gulf, the Trucial States were slowly drawing themselves together into the United Arab Emirates, and the British garrison was about to withdraw, the Corps being represented in Sharjah by elements of 15 Field Support Squadron and 53 Construction Squadron, an airfield squadron recently returned from the Caribbean.

Farther south in the Arabian Peninsula, communist dissidents in the province of Dhofar were causing trouble for the Sultanate of Oman. The Sultan had only recently succeeded his father and was trying to modernize the country. As part of a long-standing treaty with Britain, he was able to call on military help. Because he had no Sappers in his armed forces, steps were quickly taken to form and train them by instructors from Chatham. Meanwhile British units were attached for specific tasks. Artisan tradesmen were also needed to maintain the airfield at Salalah, and at first they were detached from the squadron at Sharjah. Eventually a Military Works Area was set up to run Works Services at Salalah until the Sultan prevailed in 1976.

In 1971, as a result of an extended trial carried out by 23 Amphibious Engineer Squadron with the French Gillois and German M2 amphibians, 28 Amphibious Engineer Regiment was formed in the British Army of the Rhine, operating M2B amphibians. These self-propelled rigs, which were strong enough to carry a Main Battle Tank, permitted very fast bridging of wet gaps and could also be coupled together to act as rafts for ferrying. At about the same time 59 Field Squadron became 59 Independent Commando Squadron RE

HM The Queen on an M2 amphibious ferry on a visit to Hameln in November 1993.

and was permanently affiliated to 3rd Commando Brigade, Royal Marines. All ranks have to pass the all-arms commando course, success on which is shown by the award of the green beret and the wearing of a commando dagger arm-badge.

For the Airfield Squadrons the early 1970s saw more attention being given to the techniques of rapid runway repair. This was becoming a NATO priority because of the Warsaw Pact's perceived ability to attack airfield runways and prevent aircraft taking off. Techniques were developed and materials stockpiled for repair procedures that were to become collectively known as Airfield Damage Repair. This consisted of two strands: the repair of aircraft operating-surfaces in order that aircraft could take off and land on bomb-damaged pavements; and restoration of essential services and facilities in order that the infrastructure of airfields could continue to operate and thus support the flying mission. Later, as the threat became greater, some Territorial Army units were specifically formed to carry out this task on UK main operating bases.

Also at this time came the need to support the RAF's Harrier Force. The Harrier was the first practical fixed-wing combat aircraft that had the ability for vertical/short take-off and landing. Its introduction into the RAF called for Royal Engineer ground-support in the form of operating platforms, field hides and field storage for aviation fuel. This became the responsibility of field squadrons within 38 Engineer Regiment. Having been involved in the origins of the RAF, the Corps thus had a continuing part in its flying operations, the combat engineers joining the surveyors, who have long been responsible for air navigation

data as well as land maps. In 1970, some soldiers of the Corps were also involved in flying in a different way. The concept of Independent Air Troops, where perhaps two helicopters had been allocated to regimental formations, had proved unworkable, so it was decided that the Army Air Corps would be reorganized on a regimental system like the rest of the army. The 3rd Division Aviation Regiment was formed at Netheravon, and each of its Squadrons was manned (in terms of ground staff, but with some pilots) by the major Corps. 653 Aviation Squadron was manned by a Royal Engineer ground staff (and also two RE pilots, Captain Anthony Howgate and Sergeant Ronald Young) until 1973, when, the trial having been deemed successful, the whole of the Army Air Corps was remodelled. The more senior RE personnel in 653 Squadron returned to the Corps, but most of the juniors rebadged and continued flying as observers and air gunners. During its time as an RE Squadron, 653 served two tours in Northern Ireland and provided air support to many of the regular RE units also serving there.

The origin of the soldiers of the Corps was celebrated in 1972. On 6 March, exactly 200 years since the raising of the first Company of Soldier Artificers, the Honorary Freedom of the City of Gibraltar was bestowed upon the Corps at a ceremony held in Casemates Square, Gibraltar.

In the UK, 1972 saw the disappearance of the geographical Army Commands set up by Haldane in 1904. Administrative Districts remained, but command of the field army was vested in the new Headquarters United Kingdom Land Forces. Command of the British Army of the Rhine remained at Rheindahlen, in West Germany. Another change of title occurred in 1976 when Field Squadrons (Airfields) became Field Squadrons (Construction), maintaining a broadly similar role.

Also in 1976 Her Majesty the Queen laid the foundation-stone for the new barracks to house the Training Regiments RE at Hawley, opposite Minley Manor, which had since 1972 been the Officers' Mess of the Training Regiments. This was to be named Gibraltar Barracks after the historic, but now demolished, Royal Engineer barracks in Aldershot, and also to perpetuate the long association of the Corps with Gibraltar. On completion, the barracks was formally opened on 27 September 1979 by General Sir William Jackson, GCB, KCB, MC, the Governor and Commander-in-Chief of Gibraltar, accompanied by Sir Joshua Hassan, CBE, MVO, QC, JP, the Chief Minister of Gibraltar. By coincidence, General Jackson, originally a Royal Engineer officer, had been Quartermaster General at the MOD and responsible for giving authority for the barracks to be built. The year afterwards, in 1977, HM the Queen marked the 25th anniversary of her accession to the throne. The Silver Jubilee celebrations included a Review of the Army, and it was decided that this would be held in Germany at the Sennelager Training Centre. 4th Armoured Division formed the parade and static display, while most Royal Engineer units in Germany were involved to a greater or lesser extent in preparing the site for the parade and for some 25,000 spectators.

Cap badge of the new Queen's Gurkha Engineers.

In 1977, the Queen granted the title The Queen's Gurkha Engineers to the Gurkha Engineers that had been formed in 1948. 1978 saw the Military Works Force come into being, although its origins really lay with the transfer of Works Services' responsibilities from the Corps in the early 1960s. It brought together the various Specialist Teams Royal Engineers as a civil, mechanical and electrical engineering consultancy service to HM Forces worldwide. Such technical expertise was requested by the Saudi Arabian National Guard for officers and technicians to superintend the construction of two large hospitals and a royal residence in that country by a foreign engineering consortium. In Gibraltar, the Fortress Squadron RE became 1 Fortress STRE. For combat engineers the first Combat Engineer Tractor came into service.

The decade had begun with a change in the appearance of the British soldier, when the colour of his combat suit changed from green to a camouflage-patterned cloth called Disruptive Pattern Material. Although events in Northern Ireland continued to dominate activities throughout the army, the Sappers were also called upon to use their skills in various parts of the world in the relief of natural disasters such as those caused by hurricanes, earthquakes and floods. Bomb Disposal, more correctly called Explosive Ordnance Disposal, were still on call at home and abroad, dealing with terrorist devices and ordnance remaining from the Second World War and other conflicts.

THE SOUTH ATLANTIC

On 2 April 1982, in a long-standing claim to sovereignty, the invasion by Argentina of the British possessions of the Falkland Islands and South Georgia precipitated Operation 'Corporate', the South Atlantic campaign. Within three days of the fall of the Falkland Islands, a Naval Task Force sailed from the United Kingdom with 3rd Commando Brigade, which included 59 Independent Commando Squadron. Later, 5 Infantry Brigade joined the Task Force. The other main Royal Engineer units deployed were:

RHQ and Workshop 36 Engineer Regiment
9 Parachute Squadron with a troop of 20 Field Squadron under command
11 Field Squadron for Harrier Support
61 Field Support Squadron

In addition to warships, the cruiseships, *Queen Elizabeth 2* and *Canberra*, were taken into use as troopships. The Falklands are 13,000 kilometres from the UK, so Ascension Island, another British possession almost midway between the African and South American continents, was used as a Forward Mounting Base for ships and aircraft. A troop from 51 Field Squadron (Construction) and 516 Specialist Team RE (Bulk Petroleum) deployed rapidly to the island to prepare accommodation and lay fuel pipelines.

Apart from the units already mentioned in the Task Force, Explosive Ordnance Disposal, Postal, and Military Works Force units were also well represented, but Royal Engineer involvement was in top gear from

"Sappers have to be good soldiers. They must be able to survive in combat, to handle their weapons confidently, and to look after themselves in arduous conditions. All this, and be good combat engineers and tradesmen too! Sappers were, quite literally, everywhere during the campaign. They were right up the front in every battle clearing mines; some were serving with or took part in Special Forces operations; they off-loaded ships and provided water transport; they dealt with unexploded bombs on ships; they built Harrier strips and bulk fuel systems for the Royal Navy, the Army and Royal Air Force; they ran power stations and water treatment plants; they repaired buildings; they built bridges; and they fought as infantry. There is no doubt in my mind that the Arm which displayed the greatest flexibility, resourcefulness and initiative was the Royal Engineers. We proved that we could perform most other Arms' roles at least as well as they could. I was tremendously proud of the achievements of the Sappers during and after the campaign. And we, as a Corps, can be proud too."
– Commander Royal Engineers,
Lieutenant Colonel G. W. Field, MBE, RE

the very first day because of the need to produce up-to-date mapping. Military Survey was able to produce the necessary maps for all three services in a very short time despite a shortage of current data.

59 Independent Commando Squadron, with 2 Troop 9 Parachute Squadron under command, were in the vanguard of the amphibious assault landings on the Falklands on 21 May 1982, which were met by a heavy counterattack from the Argentine Air Force. 11 Field Squadron landed on 24 May to build a Harrier strip but lost most of its equipment when the stores ship, the SS *Atlantic Conveyor*, was sunk. Nevertheless,

The Airstrip at San Carlos.

a workable strip and fuel installation was open by 5 June. 5th Infantry Brigade landed in early June to join 3rd Commando Brigade. The commandos then 'yomped' over 80 kilometres in harsh weather and terrain, much of it on foot, to retake Port Stanley, the capital.

The Argentinians surrendered on 14 June, some 25 days after the initial landings. As so many times before at the end of campaigns, the Sappers then had to take out their toolboxes and start reconstruction. Tasks such as repair of the main airfield, which had been bombed by the RAF to deny its use, restoration of water and electrical supplies, and provision of accommodation for the garrison were immediately put in hand. To cope with all of this a Military Works Area was declared, and fresh troops in the shape of 60 Field Support Squadron were sent south.

Explosive Ordnance Disposal also became very prominent because of the need for battle-area clearance to minimize casualties from Argentine minefields and unexploded ordnance from the fighting. Essential areas were cleared by 49 EOD Squadron, but, to avoid even more casualties, other areas were marked and fenced off. However, in the immediate aftermath of the campaign, nearly two million items of unexploded ordnance of over 60 different types were dealt with.

Unusually for the army, in the campaign two members of the Corps were awarded naval decorations for gallantry. Warrant Officer 2 J. H. Phillips, RE, and Staff Sergeant J. Prescott, RE, both of 49 EOD Squadron, were tasked to deal with an unexploded bomb in the boiler room of HMS *Argonaut* on 22 May 1982. Another unexploded bomb lay in a flooded missile-magazine near by. Working in extraordinarily cramped conditions and in very unfamiliar surroundings, they rendered the bomb safe, and it was later removed

The DSC medal group of WO2 Phillips.

bomb safe using a remote method. After a fourth attempt, the bomb unexpectedly exploded, blowing in a fully clipped steel door. Staff Sergeant Prescott died instantly and Warrant Officer 2 Phillips was seriously injured. Both men had displayed courage of the highest order in persevering with attempts to defuse the bomb in *Antelope*, fully aware that its condition was particularly dangerous.

from the ship. This allowed the boiler room to be repaired so that *Argonaut* regained propulsion. The following day Warrant Officer 2 Phillips and Staff Sergeant Prescott were tasked to neutralize two unexploded bombs in HMS *Antelope*. The first bomb they came to could not be approached until extensive debris had been cleared. They therefore set about making safe the second bomb, which had been slightly damaged and was assessed as being in a dangerous condition. They tried three times to render this

Warrant Officer 2 Phillips was awarded the Distinguished Service Cross, an award for officers and warrant officers of the Royal Navy and awarded for acts of gallantry in the face of the enemy. It is believed to be the first to a member of the Corps of Royal Engineers. Staff Sergeant Prescott was posthumously awarded the Conspicuous Gallantry Medal, a very rare naval award for petty officers and ratings of the Royal Navy. The award to Staff Sergeant Prescott was the first to be made to either the army or the RAF and the first during the reign of HM Queen Elizabeth II.

MAJOR CHANGES
AND THE END OF THE COLD WAR

Back at home, and in the British Army of the Rhine, a reorganization plan was being put in hand for all the Defence Forces as a general updating process. Being in support of all three Services, the Corps was involved in varying degrees. One small effect of this was the decision that Royal Naval and Royal Engineer diving training should be co-located and so the Royal Engineers Diving Establishment moved from its home at the old military port of March-

wood to HMS *Vernon* at Portsmouth.

'RE 200' was the theme for 1987, because in that year the Corps celebrated two things – the 200th anniversary of

"Mr Gorbachev, open this gate ... tear down this wall." –
US President
Ronald Reagan

the granting of the 'Royal' title to the officers of the Corps of Engineers, and the formation in England of the Royal Military Artificers, a body of engineer soldiers to

complement those of the Soldier Artificer Company already established on Gibraltar. The Corps was honoured by a visit to Chatham by HM The Queen, our Colonel-in-Chief, and by furnishing the guard on Buckingham Palace and St James's Palace by 9 Parachute Squadron. A Thanksgiving Service in St Paul's Cathedral and a concert of music in the Royal Albert Hall in London were just two events held worldwide to mark these anniversaries.

Towards the end of the decade a squadron was raised in the Channel Islands funded by the States (or government) of Jersey. The full title of this Territorial Army unit is The Jersey Field Squadron Royal Engineers (The Royal Militia of the Island of Jersey). It will be recalled that in 1806 the Companies of the Royal Military Artificers were numbered, and the 8th Company was split between Jersey and Guernsey. When first raised, the squadron was employed in supporting the Royal Air Force, but it is now part of the Royal Monmouthshire Royal Engineers (Militia).

In the 1980s, the appearance of the British soldier changed again with the introduction of more modern equipment, much of it relating to lessons learned in Operation 'Corporate', the Falklands campaign. Improved cold- and wet-weather equipment was introduced, and clothing containing man-made fibres was withdrawn – when it caught fire it melted on to the skin, causing severe burns. The steel helmet, dating from 1915, disappeared, and a new combat helmet made from Kevlar was issued. The 1984-pattern combat suit included improvements recommended after the Falklands campaign, and the combat high-boot became standard. Issues also began of a new small-arms weapon system called SA80. A NATO agreement had settled on a 5.56mm-calibre cartridge but not on a universal weapon. The British army introduced a new British individual weapon to replace both the self-loading rifle and submachine-gun, and a new light support-weapon to replace the BREN light machine-gun.

The 1980s ended with dramatic events changing the structure of Europe that had existed since the end of the Second World War in 1945. Negotiations had been in hand for some time between the superpowers of the United States and the Soviet Union to lessen the grip of the Cold War and reduce the potential for its escalation into armed conflict. However, growing unrest in the civilian populations, internal political pressure and economic weakness in Russia and its Eastern European satellites brought about a rapid collapse of the Warsaw Pact at the end of the 1980s. Poland, Hungary and Czechoslovakia threw off the Russian yoke, and Romania ousted its communist dictator in 1989. Not least, East Germany also rejected its Russian overlords and later elected to be reunited with West Germany.

These changes had a most profound effect, and the last decade of the 20th century began with a review of defence requirements to meet the changed military posture necessary to face the new world order.

OPTIONS FOR CHANGE AND THE STRATEGIC DEFENCE REVIEW

In the 1990s, the armed forces of the United Kingdom underwent the most radical change they had experienced since the Second World War. The signal for this was a review by the Secretary of State for Defence that the government would be examining all options for change – the term 'Options for Change', often colloquially shortened to 'Options', became a catchphrase for all the changes that occurred after the collapse of the Warsaw Pact. In fact, the roots of 'Options' lay further back, and its timing with the events in Eastern Europe was a coincidence.

In the years following the Falklands War, the Corps had returned to the cycle of training and projects, which had previously been its stock-in-trade. In Germany, the crucible of the Cold War, new tactical thinking to better support armoured formations was leading to greater mechanization and closer integration between armoured and field engineers, but at increased cost. This Sapper requirement was typical of the trend towards increased sophistication of equipment and weaponry that was pushing defence expenditure well above the rate of inflation.

"Life changes and this alliance, too, will be transformed. Alliances are not forever." – Soviet President Gorbachev, July 1988

Defence had been given a high priority in the Conservatives' 1979 election campaign, but the realities of government resulted in cutbacks to programmes. Equipment-cost inflation was running at five per cent, and by late 1980 the MOD was heading for an overspend. A defence review was inevitable, and a 1981 White Paper entitled 'The Way Forward' proposed changes that would leave 'the RAF better off, the army about the same and the Navy considerably worse off'. For the army, the British Army of the Rhine strength of

55,000 would be maintained. Cost savings would be achieved by reorganizing the four armoured divisions of two brigades into three divisions of three brigades, of which a divisional headquarters and one brigade would be permanently stationed in the UK.

The expected furore was pre-empted by the Falklands War and the subsequent 1983 election, which resulted in a new strategy. Support to NATO would continue, and 'Out of Area' commitments were to be recognized by greater emphasis on coordinated military assistance and by improvements in strategic mobility. The Secretary of State's more urgent priority was a reorganization of defence management. What emerged was that the Chief of Defence Staff would now speak for all three single-service chiefs. A single Vice-Chief of Defence Staff would become the channel through which four departments would report on Commitments, Systems, Policy and Programmes, and Personnel.

New cuts were introduced, justified on the grounds of efficiency, the defence share of Gross Domestic Product having fallen by 0.9 per cent between 1984 and 1988. In July 1991 the government published a White Paper entitled 'Britain's Defence for the 90s' which envisaged about a 25 per cent reduction in the armed forces by the mid-1990s. The White Paper also announced the NATO decision to create a multinational Allied Command Europe Rapid Reaction Corps under British command, the UK component of which would include an armoured division based in Germany. Two divisions would be based in the UK, one predominantly mechanized and the other air-mobile. Other measures, announced at the time, included the formation of the Adjutant General's Corps and the Royal Logistic Corps to absorb the various Corps then responsible for the administration and supply of the army. In line with the trend towards equality of the sexes, the Women's Royal Army Corps was to disband, and women were rebadged to the regiments and corps in which they were already employed. Within the Corps, women were soon to be seen in many non-combat trades.

Under 'Options', the Regular army was to be reduced to 116,000, and plans were announced in December 1991 for a Territorial Army of 63,500. The regular element of the Corps in the field army was to reduce from fifteen regiments to ten, with three brigade-affiliated close-support regiments and a fourth general-support regiment based in Germany as part of 1st (UK) Armoured Division. Six regiments would be based in the UK: one air-support, one Explosive Ordnance Disposal, a new regiment for Northern Ireland, and two close-support brigade-affiliated regiments, plus a general-support regiment for 3rd (UK) Division. These reductions were to be somewhat offset by increases in the Territorial Army. The substantial commitment the Corps now had to air-support was now to be met from three regiments, one of which (73) would take on the Harrier role, while two (76 and 77) would command the eight airfield-damage-repair squadrons. These were under the command of Headquarters 12 Engineer Brigade, which had been in existence at Waterbeach since 1982 and by 1991 had developed strong links with Headquarters Strike Command. A new regiment, (78) was to be formed to command the UK-based amphibious engineers and the field squadrons in the south of England. 29 and 30 Engineer Brigade Headquarters, which had done so much to build up the reputation, strength and professionalism of the Territorial Army in the Corps, were both victims of the changes.

One of the most far-reaching decisions for the Corps was the change to Junior Entry. The Junior Leaders Regiment RE was closed in 1990, and the Army Apprentice College at Chepstow, which had a large output to the Corps, in 1994. This ended a system that had provided the Corps with exceptionally well-trained soldiers, tradesmen and technicians and had been its backbone for many years. It had also provided a substantial proportion of the clerks of works and garrison engineers on which the Corps had depended and would need in the expeditionary army era. Luckily, it was not long before the shortsightedness of the decision to abandon a system that had been so attractive to young men of suitable skills, and so much the foundation of the technician element of the Corps, was realized. The former Army Apprentices College at Arborfield was resuscitated and, by 1998, had taken on RE Apprentice training. Junior Entry now operates in the Army Foundation College at Harrogate.

Another decision directly affecting the Corps was to streamline logistic support for the army by amalgamating the existing Royal Corps of Transport, Royal Army Ordnance Corps, Royal Pioneer Corps and Army Catering Corps into a new Royal Logistic Corps. Included in this was the Postal and Courier Service RE. This specialized branch had been formed in 1882 from Post Office employees and provided an efficient postal and telegraph service in the South African

War. In 1908 they were organized into Royal Engineers (Postal Section) and in the Great War increased in strength from 300 in 1914 to 7,000 in 1918. After the First World War and service in the occupied Rhineland, the section withered to a reserve force of 15 officers and 250 soldiers found from the Territorial Force RE. The outbreak of the Second World War required expansion of the service again, mostly by mobilized post office employees. By 1945 the strength had once again reached 7,000, and detachments of the RE Postal Service were to be found in all theatres of war, taking part in assault landings and establishing field post offices within hours. After 1945 the lessons of the morale value of regular mail had been well learned, and the postal service remained part of the Regular army. Detachments making use of the most modern methods of sorting and transporting mail were to be found wherever British troops were deployed. In 1953 the Army Postal Service took over the transmission of classified mail by courier, and its title changed to the Royal Engineers Postal and Courier Service. This had often been a target for rationalization, but it had never been possible to prove that there would be any great savings from such a move. In the event, in April 1993 the Postal and Courier Service left the Corps and rebadged into the new Royal Logistic Corps, as indeed the Transportation Branch had done in 1965 with the then newly formed Royal Corps of Transport.

By this stage, it seemed that the limit had been reached on reorganizations and reductions in capability to meet the politico-military requirements of the post-Warsaw-Pact era. However, by the time of the arrival of the new Labour government

Sleigh Post by Terence Cuneo.

in May 1997, the assumptions of 'Options for Change' were already beginning to look suspect, particularly in the light of the expeditionary posture that had started with the Gulf War in 1991. In July 1998 the new Secretary of State initiated another defence review that was to lead to yet more studies and the Strategic Defence Review, implementation of which began almost immediately. Summarizing the situation in his 1998 annual report to the Corps, Brigadier A. E. Whitley, the Engineer-in-Chief, made the following comment:

'Within an expeditionary era, the Royal Engineers have a key role before, during and after any conflict. But the Strategic Defence Review is unlikely to provide the final solution. We have not yet tied our military engineering in with likely future allies, nor attempted to address any common

weaknesses in conjunction with them; an illustration is the more robust wide river crossing capability of other armies which we might need to use in some future campaign. Neither have we fully addressed the opportunities offered by our manifold contributions to defence diplomacy. Further changes are inevitable, not only with the delivery of military capability, but right across defence.'

The essence of the Strategic Defence Review was support to NATO, the maintenance of an effective capability for intervention overseas (with the main emphasis on the Gulf, the Near East and North Africa) and a reduction in emphasis on home defence. A reform of the procurement system was also to be initiated. The most controversial measure was the reduction of the Territorial Army on the basis that the requirement for home defence, as understood during the Cold War, had greatly reduced. Reserves would, however, still be required to make up unit establishments on operational deployments.

The overall strength of Britain's regular armed forces was to be increased, but this would be at the expense of the Territorial Army, which would reduce to just over 41,000. In principle this review was to be 'foreign-policy-led' rather than simply a Treasury-driven cost-cutting exercise and envisaged a capability for intervention overseas, including in the Near and Middle East, normally as part of a multinational force. This in itself necessitated greater emphasis on joint operations and rationalization between the services in the interests of interoperability. The intervention capability was to be realized through the Joint Rapid Reaction Force, developing the reinforced brigade-sized Joint Rapid Deployment Force and Permanent Joint Headquarters concept introduced in 1997. The nature of expeditionary-type operations in the Gulf and the Balkans had proved beyond doubt that the ability to mount such future operations effectively was likely to depend heavily on a robust military engineering capability. The long battle for the Corps to be equipped to work alongside armour was being won. What emerged from the Strategic Defence Review was based on the principle that Sapper support to brigades should be provided at the scale of a close-support squadron to a battle group. In 1st (UK) Division, based in Germany for the foreseeable future, all Sapper squadrons would be for close-support. In 3rd (UK) Division, based in the UK, the available assets would only allow for one close-support and two mechanized squadrons in each regiment.

There were to be significant increases in other areas as well. In September 1999, 5 Airborne Brigade, which had been established as a consequence of 'Options', amalgamated with 24th Airmobile Brigade to form 16th Air Assault Brigade. For this, a new regiment (23) was formed based on 51 Field Squadron (redesignated 'Air Assault') and 9 Parachute Squadron. As it happened, the first commander of the new 16th Air Assault Brigade was a Sapper, Brigadier Peter Wall, a former OC of 9 Parachute Squadron. Air support was to be provided by newly formed regular squadrons, 33 Engineer Regiment (EOD) was to be enhanced, and the Military Works Force self-sustainability was to be improved. Overall, the effect of the Strategic Defence Review on the Corps was a 13 per cent increase in regular manpower and a 20 per cent increase in the number of sub-units.

Much of these enhancements were at the expense of the Territorial Army, which, for the Sappers, reduced by 56 per cent. Specialists particularly were retained in the shape of seven Specialist Teams RE, two regiments allocated to air-support and one retained for EOD. Perhaps the most forward-looking change was the reintroduction of a brigade headquarters, 29 (Corps Support) Engineer Brigade, albeit under the command of a colonel, to provide command and control for Corps engineer troops for the Allied Rapid Reaction Corps. The new brigade had command in peacetime over the units that would be assigned to the Allied Rapid Reaction Corps in war and over the Military Works Force (V) and Civil Affairs Group (V). In war it would function as a Reaction-Corps-roled multinational engineer brigade, taking on a Dutch and an Italian battalion in addition to its own organic units.

However, as we shall see later in this history, more changes were afoot in the new millennium, in the form of the Future Army Structure.

WAR IN THE MIDDLE EAST

In August 1990 the Middle East again erupted, this time in the Persian Gulf. Iraq invaded and occupied Kuwait, to which there was an immediate United Nations response, particularly as Saudi Arabia also appeared threatened. Other Arab nations and NATO countries offered troops or logistic support to what became Coalition Forces under overall US command. For the United Kingdom, Operation 'Granby' was the largest deployment of troops since 1945. The British army component was 1st Armoured Division from Germany, soon to be nicknamed the 'Desert Rats' after their predecessors in Eighth Army's desert campaign of 1942.

They began landing in Saudi Arabia in the autumn of 1990 with, initially, 21 Engineer Regiment in support, followed by 23 Engineer Regiment and 32 Armoured Engineer Regiment. 39 Engineer Regiment from the UK were also in place to prepare the British army and RAF bases, and in this they were assisted by detachments from Explosive Ordnance Disposal, the Military Works Force, Survey and Postal. As in the Falklands campaign in 1982, the Survey Branch was heavily involved from the very first. The need for maps, overlays, air-navigation charts and moving map displays was immense, not only in surveying, but updating existing maps and the actual printing of

21 Engineer Regiment laying anti-tank mines.

maps and charts. In about four mouths, 16,000,000 sheets were produced, using up 600 tonnes of paper. Once again the Corps was fulfiling its traditional role in helping the army and RAF to fight, to move and to live and preparing for an armoured battle in a potential nuclear, biological and chemical environment. But the war was to be in the desert for the first time since the Second World War, and this meant adapting equipment or obtaining new items at short notice, and quickly gaining expertise in their operation. The art of navigation in a featureless desert also had to be relearned, and the Corps ran courses for all-comers.

In this so-called 'Gulf War', units were brought to their war establishments by reinforcement from other regular units (and some Territorial) in the UK and Germany, so a named unit would inevitably include personnel from other units; thus most units of the Corps were represented, if only by an individual. All units in Cyprus were also involved in direct support, including 62 Cyprus Support Squadron.

By the end of the year constant strategic attacks by Coalition Air Forces were being made on Iraq. The land battle started on 24 February 1991 and within 100 hours victory was achieved, and the Iraqi forces were comprehensively defeated. As ever, the Corps was immediately at work on rehabilitation, one of the first jobs in liberated Kuwait City being the restoration of plumbing and electrical services to the British Embassy by 53 Field Squadron (Construction), with 49 EOD Squadron being fully committed to mine- and other bomb-disposal. The usual Battle Area Clearance followed, and 36 Engineer Regiment was sent out to assist.

In April 1991 Operation 'Haven' was mounted as a multinational force to assist in providing safe havens for the victimized Kurds in northern Iraq. 3rd Commando Brigade was tasked as the main British element, with 59 Independent Commando Squadron RE as their engineer support. In addition 51 Field Squadron, elements of 6 Field Support Squadron and 524 STRE (Works) were also deployed in traditional Sapper tasks, particularly water supply, sanitation, Explosive Ordnance Disposal and setting up of camps.

THE BALKANS

In May 1992, 1 Troop, 3 Field Squadron, arrived in Croatia to support the small United Nations force that was there primarily to enforce the demilitarization of the four United Nations protected areas of Knin, Toprska, Daruvar and Vukovar. The troop's immediate tasks were improving accommodation for 24 Field Ambulance Group in Zagreb and the construction and

"In the event that the situation had deteriorated and a break-in operation into Sarajevo ... had become necessary then armoured engineers would have been the lead element. Once again we are reminded that there comes a time in war when Sappers have to go in front to open up the way. 'Follow the Sapper' is a timeless cry." – Brigadier I. T. D. McGill's Report to the Corps, 1995

refurbishment of medical section accommodation and working facilities in each of the protected areas. Within eight weeks the troop was widely in demand elsewhere in the disintegrating Yugoslav nation, particularly in support of the United Nations headquarters and units in Sarajevo. So began a commitment that has dominated Corps life throughout the remaining period of this history.

Yugoslavia was a Western-leaning communist state in Eastern Europe and not part of the Soviet Union's sphere of influence. Following the death of Tito, Yugoslavia's benevolent dictator, multi-party elections ended communist rule in the former Yugoslavian republics of Croatia and Slovenia, and both republics declared their independence. The Serb-dominated Federal Government of Yugoslavia had taken unsuccessful military action to halt Slovenia's independence and then tried to prevent a similar occurrence in Croatia. By late 1991 fighting in Croatia had deadlocked, and in January 1992 the Serbs accepted international mediation on behalf of the United Nations. This resulted in the protected areas in which 3 Field Squadron was already busy. However, an unsatisfactory territorial split remained a bone of contention between the factions, and the UN presence developed into a 14,000-strong peacekeeping force operating in Croatia, composed principally of Canadian and French troops, with its headquarters in Sarajevo.

Whereas Croatia and Slovenia had received international recognition as independent states in January 1992, Bosnia-Herzegovina was not considered viable as an independent state. Bosnian Serbs had already taken steps to protect their status, and, in support, the largely Serb-led Federal army had increased its presence. By early 1992 heavy artillery positions had been constructed around many Bosnian towns as federal troops withdrew into Bosnia from Croatia. Accordingly, the Muslim and non-Serb community of Bosnia felt threatened with absorption into a 'Greater Serbia', and the mixed-ethnic, Muslim-led government held a referendum on independence in February 1992. Their leaders forbade Bosnian Serbs to vote, and every effort was made to enforce this, but some 64 per cent of the population did vote and almost unanimously backed the proposition of an independent Bosnia-Herzegovina, with equality to Muslim, Serb and Croat citizens. Bosnia thus seceded from Yugoslavia, and a civil war broke out in which the Bosnian Serbs were sustained by the actions of the Yugoslav Federal army. By the end of 1992, Bosnia-Herzegovina was in near chaos. Communities that had coexisted since 1945 were fighting each other with hatred and brutality, and pressure grew for intervention by the international community. The particular concern was for Sarajevo, where the Muslim population was resisting Serb efforts to take control of the city, with potentially dire consequences for the Muslim population. Relief was urgently needed, and to that end, in the autumn of 1992, a United Nations Protection Force was mandated to establish an infrastructure and protection force, which could provide relief for the population in northern Bosnia. It was into the melting-pot of the former Republic of Yugoslavia that the army was precipitated in November 1992, acting as part of the protection force.

The initial deployment on this, Operation 'Grapple 1', was from 35 Engineer Regiment, together with 519 Specialist

Team Royal Engineers (Works), which provided the close- and general-support to 1 Cheshire's battle group. Bosnia was to pose some daunting challenges to the military engineer. The weather was appalling, varying from a scorching 30°C to −10°C with a wind-chill down to −40°C and up to two metres of snow. Communications were difficult in an area ravaged by fighting. The topography was mountainous, and the lines of communication to the Croatian base of Split were some 200 kilometres long. Added to this, the army was never really sure who the enemy was.

Much of 35 Engineer Regiment's contribution in the operational area was complemented by a Geographic team of some 20 officers and soldiers based at the headquarters of the United Nations Protection Force in Zagreb, Croatia, Bosnia-Herzegovina Command at Kiseljak in Bosnia and HQ British Forces at Split in Croatia. Their role was to provide geographical planning support, terrain analysis and graphics in the headquarters, updated tactical situation maps and an in-theatre map-supply system.

After 35 Engineer Regiment's departure in May 1993, military engineer support to the battalion group was reduced to a single squadron, enhanced to some 250 strong, despite concerns within the Corps that the complex setting of such an operation required a regimental level of command. 1 Field Squadron undertook Operation 'Grapple 2' with 521 STRE (Well Drilling), who were tasked to solve the water-supply problem for British Protection Force units, productive boreholes being located at Vitez, Gornji Vakuf, Tomislavgrad and (for the Dutch) at Busovaca, thus relieving these bases of dependence on unreliable local supplies. 11 Field Squadron followed on Operation 'Grapple 3', but it was soon appreciated that a single field squadron was insufficient to provide the necessary support to the force, and the tactical headquarters of 38 Engineer Regiment deployed in February 1994 to help relieve the pressure on a single squadron. At this point, meeting the Bosnia commitment coincided with the process of drawdown following 'Options for Change'. Problems resulting from overstretch were most serious in the small trade groups, where individuals found themselves committed to back-to-back operational tours with only weeks between

them. Understandably, this had morale and retention implications.

From April 1994 to August 1995, the Operations 'Grapple 4, 5, 6 and 7' commitment was met by an engineer regiment of two field squadrons, a field support (or HQ) squadron, STRE (Works) and a troop from 33 Engineer Regiment (EOD), a total establishment of 400. By this time the UN Protection Force's operational area had been divided into three sectors, the British contribution being located in Sector Southwest with a small RHQ co-located with Sector Headquarters at Gornji Vakuf. The regiment was known as BRITENGBAT. The regiment's work was divided between giving close-support to the British units (two infantry battalions and a reconnaissance regiment) and more general support throughout the sector. BRITENGBAT represented some 40 per cent of engineer effort in the sector and possessed the only capability in specializations such as heavy plant, diving, design and EOD. First priority was the security of protection force units and personnel, which involved protection work in the unit bases and also led to numerous EOD tasks. For example, nearly 3,000 mines or unexploded ordnance were disposed of in 21 Engineer Regiment's tour of duty during Operation 'Grapple 6'. Dealing with the widespread mines problem was a continuing commitment. Monitoring the work of the clearance and marking teams and contributing to mines awareness training was of utmost importance in meeting the aims of the UN Protection Force. The construction and maintenance of camps also remained a significant task. For example, during Operation 'Grapple 5', the regiment built 3 camps and was responsible for maintaining 13, which included the winterization of British units' accommodation and offices. Also central to the UN mission was the reconstruction of civilian facilities, generally known as G5 Infrastructure Projects. This type of work, restoring power or water supplies, refurbishing hospitals and schools and repairing local road networks, was crucial to the settlement of communities and to discouraging them from taking up arms again in intercommunal violence.

The political and military circumstances arrived at in mid-1995 opened a window of opportunity for peace talks. By then the Serb position in Bosnia had deteriorated. UN sanctions had reduced the extent to which the Serbs were able to support their Bosnian brothers, and the Bosnian Croats had built up their military strength and re-established an alliance with the Muslims. These factors, together with the United States involvement in airstrikes, were an indication to all parties that realistically there was no further room for manoeuvre. Hence the Dayton Peace Accord, following talks between the Yugoslav Federation, the Bosnian Muslims and the Croatians, signed on 14 December 1995. The accord agreed that the sovereign state known as the Republic of Bosnia and Herzegovina was to consist of two entities: the Bosnian Serb Republic and the Federation of Bosnia, with an agreed boundary line between them. The accord was to be guaranteed by the deployment of an International Implementation Force, to be known as Operation 'Joint Endeavour'. The UN authorized NATO to provide this at a force level of 55,000 troops, of which 8,400 were British, whose contribution was known as Operation 'Resolute'. In accordance with the Peace Accord, the Implementation Force was to undertake the following primary military tasks:

To ensure continued compliance with the ceasefire.

The separation of forces and their withdrawal from the agreed ceasefire zone of separation back to their respective territories.

The collection of heavy weapons into cantonment sites and barracks, and the demobilization of remaining forces.

For the Royal Engineers, the Implementation Force represented an increase in tempo. The land element was commanded by Headquarters Allied Command Europe Rapid Reaction Corps. It comprised three multinational divisions, Multinational Division South-West being allocated to the UK. The first formation appointed to this task was 3rd (UK) Division, which commanded two brigades, 4th (UK) Armoured Brigade and a Canadian brigade, both of which had their own Sappers. In the case of 4th Armoured Brigade, 32 Engineer Regiment provided the brigade's close support while 38 Engineer Regiment with 527 STRE (Works) and elements of 49 Field Squadron (EOD), already in theatre on Operation 'Grapple 7', provided the divisional general support. The urgency of the deployment and the massive flow of tasks needed in a devastated country demonstrated the need for an efficient and flexible resources system. Although there was a system in existence at the start of Operation 'Reso-

lute', the current incumbent unit, 15 Field Park Squadron, had to adapt rapidly to cope with the new situation. Particularly important was demand for quarried stone and aggregate. A pan-Bosnia plan was devised to restore quarries, brick factories, cement and other building-supply industries, in which Royal Engineer technicians took an influential part. Fortunately the Corps policy of maintaining a capability for quarrying in the training syllabus, a lesson learned from the Falklands, proved its worth.

Operation 'Resolute 2' began in mid-1996 with the deployment of 36 Engineer Regiment and 22 Engineer Regiment. The level of activity provided the Corps with some challenges in nominating units for these commitments. As noted earlier, tour lengths and the intervals between tours were now becoming critical considerations, bearing on the morale of soldiers with possible long-term consequences for retention. In his August 1997 report, Brigadier I. T. D. McGill, the Engineer-in-Chief, gave the tour interval in the previous year as 'between eleven and twelve months, but this is set to rise to twenty-one months by the middle of 1998 if no unforeseen commitments arise'. The changeover saw a move towards civil-aid works such as bridges, water and electricity supply, but the camp-building programme continued apace, particularly on what became known as the Hilltop Sites containing remote rebroadcast stations.

The Corps carried out two enduring and important tasks throughout the Bosnia campaign. EOD personnel, or dedicated mines-awareness teams, had carried out Mines Awareness Training in the theatre for

MAMBA bomb disposal vehicle in the Balkans.

some time. All Implementation Force personnel arriving at Banja Luka or Split received a mines-awareness brief from an EOD officer or senior NCO. In addition, units, visiting non-government organizations, school teachers and children were so briefed. Operation 'Resolute' had also brought a need to boost the geographic support. Essentially, the new commitment meant the deployment of 14 Independent Topographic Squadron to set up a theatre Geographic Support Group. UK military survey was to provide more than 80 per cent of the geographic support within the Implementation Force, with posts spread throughout ten different locations. The squadron comprised a production troop, map troop, support troop and a multinational topographic survey troop. The single most important task of the group was map supply, more than six million maps being

handled during the first six months of the operation.

The one-year UN Mandate for the Implementation Force was due to expire in December 1996, so a Stabilization Force replaced it. The UK contribution to this was called Operation 'Lodestar' and was about half the size of Operation 'Resolute', the Sapper element comprising a regimental headquarters acting as HQRE, two close-support squadrons, a field support or park squadron, an STRE (Works), two EOD detachments and the Geographic Support Group. All elements were placed under command of HQRE. The start of Operation 'Lodestar' coincided with the establishment of the Permanent Joint Force Headquarters, which now became responsible for mounting and sustaining the operation. Such a major reduction in the engineer force level, when set against the level of activity, caused concern for the mounting units. For 39 Engineer Regiment, the replacement for 22 Engineer Regiment, the problems were acute because the regiment was organized for an air-support role with two of its field squadrons committed to in-role deployments. The regiment set about solving its manning shortfall by appealing for volunteers from the Territorial Army and reservists, more than 80 of whom joined them for their pre-Bosnia training. On deployment in October, they relieved both 22 and 36 Engineer Regiments. In December, on transition to Operation

'Lodestar', their order of battle became RHQ, 60 HQ & Support Squadron, a Geographic detachment, EOD and elements of the Military Works Force at Banja Luka, 48 Field Squadron at Gornji Vakuf and 31 Armoured Engineer Squadron at Mrkonjic Grad, with 45 Field Support Squadron at Split and Tomislavgrad. Routine winter tasks such as route maintenance and repair, snow clearance and camp maintenance and construction were carried out in difficult and variable conditions, often below −35°F. The introduction of an automated and civilianized radio system, as a result of which a Royal Signals regiment could be released, led to the construction of rebroadcast sites, principally self-contained accommodation on very exposed, minefield-surrounded hilltops. The change in force levels also led to the stripping and handback of substantial numbers of unwanted military camps.

During the early days of both the Implementation and Stabilization Forces' mandates, the contribution of the RE chartered engineers became a real force multiplier. Very few of the NATO military contingents had such engineers, and relied to a great degree on civilian contractors. Work was therefore always reactive and dependent on a relatively benign operational situation. Only the British and the Canadians had chartered engineers in theatre, and these were always in great demand. For example, in September 1996, when the Zetra Ice Rink Stadium was proposed as the site of a temporary base for the headquarters of the Stabilization Force, the Americans demanded a full survey before they would authorize its use. This survey was carried out, and recommendations accepted, in four days.

21 Engineer Regiment followed on in March 1997. The tour was notable as the first operational tour of 65 Field Park Squadron for over 50 years. The squadron had under command a plant troop composed largely of Territorial and reservist soldiers built around a cadre provided by the Royal Monmouthshire Royal Engineers (Militia), providing many lessons on the overall capability and utility of the Territorial Army. In July 1997 the camp at Tomislavgrad was closed down and 65 Squadron redeployed to join its Resources Troop in Split, from where all second-line engineer logistics were now provided. Two more regiments (38 and 35) were to deploy before the official end of the mandate for Operation 'Lodestar' in June 1998, the Stabilization Force continuing for UK under the title of Operation 'Palatine'. It was soon to be absorbed into the dramatic events in Kosovo.

By the end of the Bosnian War, all that remained of the Republic of Yugoslavia was the Federation of Montenegro and Serbia, the latter with its two provinces of Kosovo and Vojvodina, the former identified as a possible flashpoint. While it was the historic heartland of the Serbian nation, its population was nevertheless 90 per cent ethnic Albanian. For years Kosovo had enjoyed the status of an autonomous region within Serbia, but in 1989 Kosovar Albanians were progressively removed from official positions of power and influence, being replaced by ethnic Serbs. Early in 1998 the Serbian-manned Ministry of the Interior police brutally suppressed riots in the capital of Kosovo, Pristina.

The province of Kosovo is approximately the size of Northern Ireland. It is completely surrounded by rugged, wooded hills, with peaks reaching 2,000 metres, particularly in the regions bordering Montenegro, Albania and Macedonia. Within the central region of Kosovo are two areas of relatively flat open plain at a height of 1,750 metres above sea level, separated by a rough wooded hilly area. On the plain, most of the land is agricultural. Metalled roads link main towns to many villages, but the only practicable entry route for a military force from Macedonia is along the main motorway from Skopje to Pristina, through the Kacanik defile.

The Kosovo Liberation Army had emerged in the mid-1990s as a response to human rights abuses by the Serbian authorities. The Serbian government was able, strictly correctly, to label it as a terrorist organization, but its efforts to deal with it involved disproportionate and indiscriminate violence to the civilian Kosovar Albanians. The outcome was a series of actions in which the Liberation Army goaded the Serbs, often via the Ministry of the Interior police, resulting in reprisals by the authorities. Such actions were carried out with scant regard for civilian casualties. Throughout the summer of 1998 the conflict increased and precipitated a flow of refugees from Kosovo. Eventually, the architect of the Dayton Peace Accord, US Ambassador Holbrook, returned to the Balkans armed with the threat of renewed NATO military action against the Serbs. This threat was hamstrung by the fact that intervention in Kosovo could be seen as intervention in the internal affairs of a sovereign state; nevertheless, the Serbs were told what air strikes would involve. The outcome was an agreement that Yugoslavia would accept an unarmed mission to verify the state of the ceasefire between the Serbian army, the Ministry of the Interior police and the Kosovo Liberation Army, and eventually to oversee elections. The Kosovo Verification Mission was to be provided by the 54-nation Organization for Security and Co-operation in Europe, with the UK pledged to provide ten per cent of the mandated strength of 2,000. The mission was initially successful in reporting ceasefire violations and apportioning blame, and this acted as a brake on the violence. However, it was unable to cover the whole of Kosovo, and violence gradually escalated. After a number of early successes in the first ten weeks of the mission's operation, its position was rendered unworkable by the reprisal massacre in mid-January 1999 of some 46 civilians in the village of Racak. In the words of the Chief of Operations, Major General John Drewienkiewicz, late Royal Engineers, 'the shocking brutality of Racak … changed the landscape completely'. Military action appeared inevitable unless a political settlement could be achieved, and a conference between the two sides was held in February at Rambouillet. The Serbs refused any solution involving a NATO ground presence in sovereign Serbian territory; nor would they accept the demand of the Kosovar Albanians for complete independence. When, under pressure from NATO, that aspiration was modified to autonomy within the former Yugoslav state, NATO support for the Kosovar Albanians was guaranteed. The Serbs withdrew from negotiations and stepped up their military operations in Kosovo; the Verification Mission was expelled; and NATO bombing started on 24 March 1999. By then a campaign of ethnic cleansing had begun with a flow of refugees that became a human tide as the Kosovar Albanians, trying to escape Serb reprisals and the looting and destruction of their homes, now faced the possibility of being caught up in the bombing. When, following the devastation of his country, after three months of bombing, Slobodan Milosevic (Serbian President of Yugoslavia) finally agreed to the withdrawal of Serbian army and police units from the province, an international force, of which NATO was the predominant element, moved in on 12 June 1999. Their principal aim was to restore law and order to the province, paving the way for the return to normality.

Concurrently, military precautions had been taken. Foreseeing the possible seizure of hostages, NATO set up an extraction force to be based in Skopje. In December 1998, 20 Field Squadron and 527 STRE (Works) deployed to Macedonia in general support to the UK element of the extraction force, called Operation 'Upminster', which was based on B Company, 1 King's Own Royal Border Regiment with a troop of 11 Field Squadron in close support. Hardstandings had to be prepared for 'A' and 'B' vehicles, a building refurbished for the headquarters, four hardened aircraft shelters modified and repair and servicing facilities provided for the vehicles. This relatively routine work provided challenges enough, but, just as the end was in sight and a date fixed for the unit to return home, Operation 'Agricola' was launched. This was the concentration, at the start of the air war, of the British element of the NATO ground forces, which were to

prepare to enter Kosovo. The British element of the force was to be based on 4th Armoured Brigade with 5th Airborne Brigade allocated later to support the actual entry operation. A small HQRE was deployed from HQ 1st (UK) Armoured Division to command all engineers in theatre. 4th Armoured Brigade, whose HQ was boosted by attachments from 14 Topographic Squadron, was supported by 21 Engineer Regiment and 21 Field Squadron (EOD). Combat Services Support Group (UK), which provided the logistic support to the force and was later to be redesignated 101 Logistic Brigade, was supported by 28 Engineer Regiment and 62 CRE (Works). The latter provided, in an extremely fluid requirement environment, technical support to regiments and managed the technical and financial aspects of infrastructure engineering support to British forces, including the restoration of essential services and utilities. It comprised 527 STRE (Works) and 521 STRE (Water Development), with reconnaissance parties from 516 STRE (Bulk Petroleum) and 507 (Railways)(V), together with specialists from Defence Estates and the Engineer and Logistic Staff Corps.

Once again the lack of any Corps troops in the NATO order of battle for Kosovo bedevilled the planning process. Fortunately for the Chief Engineer, the United Kingdom had been prepared to undertake this commitment. 28 Engineer Regiment thus became responsible for general support, under 101 Logistic Brigade, while 21 Engineer Regiment provided close-support to 4th Armoured Brigade. The UK also provided all the geographic support.

28 Engineer Regiment deployed ahead of the 4th Armoured Brigade group as the enabling force and took 20 Field Squadron under command. 20 Squadron's tasking included the reconnaissance of the entire route by which the brigade were to travel from their port of disembarkation at Thessaloniki to the Kosovo border. Checking the bridge classification and upgrading bridges became a key factor with the imminent arrival of the Challenger tanks of 4th Armoured Brigade. With the start of the air war, measures had to be taken to relocate or protect vulnerable unit locations in the immediate border areas. Very soon the refugee crisis became the main effort for 28 Engineer Regiment who, with 1 Field Squadron resubordinated from 21 Engineer Regiment, now undertook the construction of camps in the Skopje area. The threat of more refugees arriving led to the deployment of 28 Engineer Regiment into Albania, where they constructed two more camps, capable of expanding to hold up to 50,000 people between them. The camps also relieved the precarious former Yugoslav government, whose support of NATO's plans was crucial, of the prospect of being swamped by this human tide.

The Durrant Bridge.

The timely arrival of a team from the Civil Affairs Group freed the squadrons of 28 Regiment to prepare for entry into Kosovo. While the bombing was in progress, the Sappers on Operation 'Agricola' were investigating in great detail the routes into the province. Apart from the classification of the bridges, which it was assessed would accept Challengers but not transporter-mounted AVREs or AVLBs, the main obstacles expected were from mines laid by any of the warring factions or demo-litions possibly created by the Serbian army. A tunnel in the Kacanik defile would not take AVLBs loaded with their bridges. This analysis of the routes enabled detailed plans to be made to overcome such difficulties and led to a successful deployment when the time came.

The NATO Kosovo ground force comprised five brigade-sized formations from France, Germany, Italy, the United Kingdom and the United States under the overall command of the British Lieutenant General Mike Jackson. The force entered the province on 12 June 1999, with the mission to secure the Kacanik defile through which 4th Armoured Brigade would advance to Pristina. The lead formation was 5th Airborne Brigade, supported by 36 Engineer Regiment. A Royal Engineers bridge-classification specialist from 62 CRE (Works) accompanied the leading troops of the road party. 5th Airborne Brigade left Kosovo in early June, their mission accomplished, but 69 Gurkha Field Squadron remained in theatre.

Sapper tasks in the immediate aftermath of the entry were aimed both at supporting their formations and restoring normality in Kosovo. At the same time, units had to guarantee their own freedom of movement, which involved route-opening and proving as well as EOD clearance, as well as the provision of traditional close engineer support to the armoured battle groups as they dominated their areas of operations. The approaching winter led an urgency to plans to provide some sort of temporary accommodation, and this quickly became one of the main efforts. Meanwhile work was required to re-establish the work force and the management structures in Pristina's utilities, such as power generation and distribution, water supply and refuse disposal.

United Nations UNPROFOR Medal.

The EOD problem was particularly acute, with vast quantities and varieties of ordnance present in the aftermath of the air war and the Serbian offensive against the Albanian population. In accordance with the then policy, all Explosive Ordnance Disposal and Improvised Explosive Device Disposal was a Sapper responsibility, as in Bosnia, but the Royal Logistic Corps and the Royal Air Force also supplied seven teams, all to work under 21 Field Squadron. It was the first time that army and Royal Air Force teams had worked together in this way. EOD specialists also dealt with mines, falling back on combat engineer support as necessary. Seven RE teams were provided for the advance into Kosovo on 12 June. The rest built up afterwards to a strength of about 100. Within three weeks they had dealt with over 1,600 tasks. In the words of the Squadron Commander, 'there were very few tasks during the first month for which EOD was not on the critical path'. Unexploded cluster sub-munitions, of which some 10 per cent had failed to explode, were a particular hazard, two members of 69 Gurkha Field Squadron, Lieutenant Gareth Evans and Sergeant Balaram Rai, being killed as they were preparing to destroy a stockpile of such munitions near a school.

Restoring the full range of utilities and essential services necessary to sustain a small country post-conflict was a new experience. There was a need for the army to replace its own field arrangements for electricity, water and sewerage as soon as possible. Equally, properly functioning utilities would be a key part in restoring some semblance of normal life to the people of Kosovo. Sappers became principally involved in power and water, but also in hospitals, prisons, the Pristina heating system, rubbish disposal, burials and fuels.

Power was a high priority, and, although the industry had not been seriously damaged in the air war, maintenance of the main generating stations had been neglected for many years and the province was dependent on imported power. The process by which the power industry was restored in Kosovo illustrates the difficulties that faced the new United Nations Mission in Kosovo. The first step was to establish who were the key personalities in the industry. They were then brought together as a committee under the chairmanship of the Chief Engineer, Allied Rapid Reaction Corps. Little by little, as confidence grew, issues were identified and the workforce reinstated. The aim was for integration on the basis of professional competence, but the murder of two Serb managers and a general loss of confidence caused the majority of Serbs to abandon their jobs. Technically it became clear that the operation of the power industry was beyond the capability of army engineers. Expert advice was called for and provided from the UK by a member of the Engineer and Logistic Staff Corps, Lieutenant Colonel R. J. Urwin, who was also a director of National Grid plc. His valuable advice launched the process by which the mission was eventually persuaded to let a management contract run the power company on a temporary basis. The appointment of Major Joe Fuller to oversee the restoration of the power station proved a lucky choice. Although he had no expertise in this area, his brother was a professional in power station management, and Major Fuller got valuable guidance and advice from him via his mobile telephone. Likewise, the soldiers of 26 Armoured Engineer Squadron had neither the training nor the expertise to run the power station but rose to the challenge

and soon won the confidence of the returning workers. There was a similar story for water supply, where the lead was taken by 521 STRE (Water Development). The Officer Commanding became Chairman of the Pristina Water Board and his 'directors' were equal numbers of Serbs and Albanians. A team recruited by the Department for International Development with a representative from Thames Water assisted. The railways, too, proved to be an important service, and, although the Italians agreed to take the lead on this matter, it was 507 STRE (Railways)(V) who produced expert advice on the condition of the permanent way. For the activation of the airfield, 53 Field Squadron (Air Support) and 529 STRE (Air Support) joined the RAF Activation Team. NATO produced the funds for restoring the essential services while those for the living arrangements and for the RAF infrastructure came from British national sources. Rubbish disposal also presented a test of Sapper ingenuity. The withdrawing Serbs had taken much of the expertise and also some of the equipment, such as the rubbish-collection vehicles, with them. Only the vehicles that could not be repaired were left behind. 26 Armoured Engineer Squadron assumed responsibility for getting the refuse disposal systems working again and soon persuaded the workforce to return to work while the squadron's fitters and plant operators repaired the remaining vehicles. Soon the mountains of rubbish littering the city streets began to disappear.

Operations in the Balkans subsequent to 1999 are covered in the chapter Into the Millennium.

TOYS FOR THE BOYS

In 2000 there was a major step forward in the engineer tank programme. The Chieftain-based range of engineer tanks, the Armoured Vehicle Launched Bridge and the Armoured Vehicle Royal Engineers, dated from the mid-1960s and by the beginning of the 21st century were showing their age. Their reliability and maintenance record was poor, and their cross-country agility was inadequate for close-support engineers to keep pace with the armoured battlegroups they supported. The introduction into service of a new engineer tank was therefore a top priority. The replacements were to be called Trojan (the replacement AVRE) and Titan (the replacement AVLB), and both versions were to be based on upgraded Challenger 2 running-gear and hulls; funding was approved for 33 of each. In 2001 a contract was let against an in-service date of 2006, and by 2004 four prototypes had completed their contractor development trials and were undergoing user trials at the RE Trials and Development Unit.

Titan is an armoured bridgelayer, which can deploy tank-bridges to cross gaps up to 24.5 metres under fire in less than two minutes. Trojan is a minefield-breacher with additional close-support characteristics. It has an 8-metre-reach excavator with 5,000kg and 2,500kg lifting-points and a 3-in-1 bucket. It is hardwired to operate Python and can carry and deploy a midifascine for anti-tank-ditch breaching. Both vehicles have a crew of three, a range of about 300 kilometres, weigh approximately 31 tonnes unloaded and mount the in-service mineplough, a dozer blade and

safe-lane route-marker system. At the same time, trials involving the mounting of a Chieftain mineplough on a Challenger 2 hull proved that it was capable of providing considerably greater performance. The Breaching and Dozing programme, which has the same in-service date as Titan and Trojan, is a replacement for the in-service mineplough and dozer blade. The programme will upgrade the Universal Dozer Kit as well as procuring a new Magnetic Signature Projector and mineplough.

In a similar timeframe, Terrier, the air-transportable replacement for the obsolete Combat Engineer Tractor, was progressing well. Terrier will have the necessary mobility to remain on station with the Warrior armoured personnel carrier and armoured protection to operate in the indirect fire-zone. It will field a multi-purpose 3-in-1 bucket system and a backhoe excavator with lift-arm attachment and be able to tow and fire Python; it is expected to enter service in 2008.

Python, a rocket-propelled explosive-hose system to breach anti-tank minefields, which was developed from the Giant Viper of the Cold War period, will be mounted on special trailers to be towed behind Trojan and Terrier and will provide further mine-breaching capability.

The Corps also benefited considerably over the period 2000 to 2005 with an equipment programme designed to update its

> *"Give us the tools and we will do the job."* –
> Churchill to the United States concerning Lend/Lease, 1941

ability for close- and general-support bridging. Air Portable Ferry Bridge is a Class 35 (Tracked) and (Wheeled) bridge/ferry system to replace the Airportable Bridge. It provides a light bridge up to 28 metres, a powered roll-on-roll-off ferry and a fly-forward bridge of up to 14 metres. The complete system is carried on a dismountable ramp-operated platform, but the basic bridge can be air-dropped from a Hercules C130 and towed on six special to role trailers behind light vehicles. The gap-crossing capability of the Close Support Bridge was improved in 2004 when the Two Span Bridge (Pontoon) was brought into service to provide an improved 62-metre crossing at Class 79 (Tracked) and Class 110 (Wheeled). The Logistic Support Bridge is based on the Mabey Johnson Compact 200 bridge. It uses proven but improved Bailey Bridge technology. An immediate stock was procured in 2001 for training and operations, with an option to procure more at short notice when required. A standard bridge set provides crossings of 58 metres at Class 80 (Tracked) and 52 metres at Class 100 (Wheeled). (The classifications given above are all Military Load Classifications.)

The critical requirement for vehicle-based mine-detection, neutralization and marking is divided into Route Proving and Reconnaissance. It is intended that a vehicle-based system called Minder (Route Proving) will provide an integrated capability to detect, neutralize and mark mines, in support of route opening and proving operations by 2006. Minder (Reconnaissance) will provide the capability for engineer reconnaissance vehicles to locate the edge of mined areas and to act as pathfinders for critical equipments by 2010.

Trojan, the replacement AVRE.

Titan, the replacement AVLB.

Terrier, the replacement Combat Engineer Tractor.

In the area of counter-mobility, specifically the use of anti-tank mines, there was considerable debate, and the success rate was mixed. In 2000 the Shielder Vehicle Launched Scatterable Mine System vehicles were delivered from industry, and the first two were fielded with 21 Engineer Regiment in Germany, fielding being completed by 2002. There appeared to be little appetite in Defence to field a new dumb-mine system to replace the Barmine, and by 2004 the Corps' counter-mobility capability was considerably eroded, by 2008 only Barmine and Shielder remaining in service. However, the Area Defence Weapon, with an in-service date of 2006, will provide a rapidly emplaced top-attack anti-tank capability for light and heavy forces and will include a remote-control capability.

A ground-breaking but contentious programme was the 'C-Vehicle Private Finance Initiative'. Its aim was to reduce the support burden of the Corps' plant fleet, much of which was mothballed in barracks, and it was expected to provide levels of reliability, availability, mobility (tactical and strategic) and survivability commensurate with the current fleet. The contract was awarded to Amey Lex Consortium in early 2005 with Full Service Provision planned for 2006.

The lack of a modern accommodation system for troops deployed on expeditionary operations was demonstrated during operations in the Balkans. A system was procured in 1999 for Kosovo, but the longer-term requirement was remedied through the Expeditionary Campaign Infrastructure programme, which was split into two tiers. Tier 1 is an early-entry capability based on a modular, soft-walled shelter system. It is fitted with climate control, containerized ablutions, fuel, water and power systems as well as catering facilities and is intended for deployments exceeding one month and generally no more than eight months, but may be in position up to a maximum of 18

months. Tier 2 is a longer-term capability with similar attributes to Tier 1. It is based on semi-permanent structures similar to those that are deployed in the Balkans. The Tier 1 programme was advanced to 2003 by an Urgent Operational Requirement to provide suitable accommodation to troops deployed on Operation 'Telic'. The deployable Engineer Workshop System provides a fully integrated modular system that gives field support squadron workshops significant additional capability, each trade group having its own area that will be designed for engineering hygiene, environmental control and flexibility to cope with the widest possible range of tasks.

The new Combat Support Boat provides support to river-crossing operations, inshore support of ship-to-shore operations including fuel supply and can act as a floating working platform for engineer tasks and for divers.

The provision of a new military digitized radio system to the army to replace the existing Clansman system introduced in the early 1980s was not without its moments. The initial Preferred Bidder was de-selected and replaced by General Dynamics (UK). 26 Engineer Regiment were the first unit to convert to the new Bowman system in early 2004, and the task of de-kitting, re-looming and fitting the new radios were a heavy commitment on regimental signals staffs. For the Corps, Bowman will also host the Engineer Battlefield Information System Application, the engineer element in the Command and Battlespace Management (Land) digitization programme. The application will provide tools to support the reconnaissance, planning, design, resourcing as well as command and control of engineer tasks in order to improve mobility, counter-mobility, survivability and sustainability support to the Joint Force.

The Corps' requirements for special-to-role and general-purpose armoured vehicles to support the new medium weight capability has been embedded in the Future Rapid Effect System programme, which will provide a Rapid Intervention and Manoeuvre Support capability and replace the army's obsolescent Saxon, FV430 series and CVR(T) vehicles from 2012. For the Corps the requirement now includes AVREs, AVLBs, Armoured Engineer Tractors and a remotely delivered mine system with an in-service date of 2014. The Future Command and Liaison Vehicle, due into service in 2007, will provide armoured and mechanized units with wheeled armoured vehicles for roles such as command, liaison and rebroadcast.

INTO THE MILLENNIUM

One might have hoped that the frenetic pace of activity that the Corps undertook in the 1990s, particularly in the Balkans, could have reduced in the new millennium, but this was not to be. The army was now a force to be used in support of foreign policy, and that meant expeditionary operations all around the world.

In 2000 the operational tempo eased, the tour interval increasing from 10 months to 13, but the pace of change continued to be fierce. The first tranche of the new Strategic Defence Review units had formed and, in the case of the UK units, deployed to the Balkans, supported in increasing numbers by members of the Royal Engineers Territorial Army, thus reinforcing the 'One Army Concept'. Manning the impressive Strategic Defence Review enhancements, which amounted to a 13 per cent increase in regular manpower and a 20 per cent increase in the number of sub-units, was not without pain, and much effort was being put into the retention at the Sapper and Junior NCO rank. The Corps was also suffering from a shortfall in soldier recruiting, which potentially compromised the enhancements.

In the Balkans, Kosovo remained the Corps' main operational effort, albeit at a reduced level. Force reductions saw 23 Amphibious Engineer Squadron and 69 Gurkha Field Squadron withdrawn in late 1999 once the majority of enabling works for the Temporary Field Accommodation project were complete. The programme resulted from the high priority that the Ministry of Defence gave the provision of good-quality semi-permanent accommodation in Kosovo, and a contract valued at approximately £110,000,000, was let by the Defence Procurement Agency with Hunting Engineering Ltd in July 1999. A twenty-man Works Project Management Team, under Lieutenant Colonel C. M. Cockerill, RE, managed the construction and subsequent acceptance

"The reputation of the Corps is gained on these (expeditionary) operations and probably stands as high now as it has ever been." – Brigadier D. R. ff. Innes, E-in-C(A), Report to the Corps, 2004

phase of this unique pathfinder contract, employing 900 UK-based and local contractors' personnel with a total monthly spend in excess of £1,500,000. Organizationally, the order of battle of a Regimental HQ, an HQ squadron, close-support squadron and field support squadron supplemented by a CRE (Works) and an Explosive Ordnance Disposal and Geographic detachment had been proved in Kosovo. 38 Engineer Regiment was replaced in the spring by 32 Engineer Regiment, which then became responsible for both Bosnia and Kosovo. 26 Engineer Regiment, which had only just reformed in Larkhill on 1 April, replaced them in August, the recently reformed 70 Gurkha Field Support Squadron being included in 26 Engineer Regiment's regimental grouping. In Bosnia, 35 Engineer Regiment withdrew early in the year, leaving 37 Field Squadron to complete their tour in March. A review of force levels reduced the UK engineer commitment to a close-support squadron seasonally adjusted to support an armoured or mechanized battlegroup, 4 Armoured Engineer Squadron being the first squadron to be deployed. 59 Independent Commando Squadron replaced them, the first time the squadron had deployed to the Balkans. Both units were heavily involved with the extension to the helicopter landing site at Banja Luka and improvements to the ammunition storage site at Glamoc. Unlike the other national engineer contingents, which only provided support to their own battlegroups, the command arrangements for the UK engineer squadron allowed it to undertake construction tasks in support of Commander Multi-National Division (South West).

In the Falkland Islands, a small maintenance section was now deployed for six months to manage and maintain engineer vehicles and equipment. In place of a permanent commitment, there was now an annual squadron-level construction project and regular in-theatre exercising of 39 Engineer Regiment's Lead Air Support Squadron to support the RAF Mount Pleasant deployed operating base. Northern Ireland continued to be a thorn in the flesh, events overtaking the initiative to rear base the Roulement Engineer Squadron in either UK or Germany, and 51 Field Squadron (Air Assault) spent much of the latter part of their tour forward-based in the province. 9 Parachute Squadron was also forward-based throughout its tour. Deconstruction took place, but increased unrest made the future uncertain.

Elsewhere, two clerks of works were deployed from Brunei to assist with the provision of power, water and other facilities to Operation 'Langar' in East Timor. Subsequently, an EOD SNCO and JNCO were joined by an electrician and plumber who provided key support to the National Contingent Command. In Sierra Leone, in response to a Non-Combatant Evacuation Operation in May, elements of the Spearhead Land Element from 20 Field Squadron and 33 Engineer Regiment (EOD), together with a Military Works Force team of key specialists, deployed as part of Operation 'Palliser'. Late in May they were replaced by a troop from 59 Independent Commando Squadron. Their role throughout was to provide field defences and simple infrastructure. Operations then switched to Operation 'Basilica', providing Short Term Training Teams to train the Sierra Leone army. RAF deployments continued to be supported by 12 (Air Support) Engineer Brigade. A small maintenance team was permanently based at each Deployed Operating Base supporting operations enforcing the Iraqi 'No Fly Zone', and teams ranged worldwide as required.

2001 saw the Corps continue to grow in size with the implementation of the Strategic Defence Review order of battle. 26 Engineer Regiment moved to its interim base at Ludgershall and, with the impending re-formation of 30 Field Squadron, was able to provide 12th Mechanized Brigade with its close-support engineer capability. The ramp-up of 23 Engineer Regiment (Air Assault) at Woodbridge commenced, and the enhancements to the Military Works Force also continued, with 518 STRE (Works) forming early in the year. The average tour interval for the Corps, even allowing for the deployment to the former Yugoslav Republic of Macedonia was now over 18 months, although certain units such as Military Works Force and 33 Engineer Regiment (EOD) suffered shorter intervals. Territorial units continued to produce a steady flow of officers and soldiers for deployment on operations, thus relieving pressure on heavily committed regular units.

In the Balkans, the pan-Balkan regimental order of battle, encompassing the Bosnia close-support squadron, and moving from one theatre to the other, and even Macedonia, as necessary, had stood the test. In late August elements of 36 Engineer Regiment deployed to Macedonia to support 16th Air Assault Brigade in the collection of weapons handed in by the Albanian-backed Kosovo Liberation Army, while 39 Armoured Engi-neer Squadron deployed from Kosovo as the Force engineer squadron. The focus in Kosovo remained upon internal security, while in Bosnia the situation was stabilizing. A close-support squadron continued to provide engineer support to both Multi-National Division (South West) and the UK battlegroup.

The reduced commitment to the Falkland Islands continued, and in Northern Ireland rear basing of the Roulement Engineer Squadron continued in principle, but not during the 'marching season'. In Sierra Leone, the RE maintenance detachment remained at an officer and ten other ranks while it supported the Short Term Training Teams. Collective training in the UK, Germany and Canada was severely restricted in the early part of the year as a result of the foot and mouth disease epidemic in England and Wales, which required plant-operators from the Corps to assist with the digging of mass graves for dead animals.

The Corps' importance as a defence asset was again demonstrated by the extensive enabling works carried out by the Corps in Oman for the Joint Rapid Reaction Force Exercise 'Saif Sareea 2', as well as the tasks undertaken during the exercise. For many units this was their main effort in 2001, which peaked in August with both 28 and 39 Engineer Regiments in theatre under the command of HQ 12th (Air Support) Engineer Brigade. The exercise, a combined joint exercise with the Sultan of Oman's armed forces, was designed to prove the Joint Rapid Reaction Force concept. Sappers supported the land, air, maritime and logistic components, and at one stage this involved significant elements of 21, 28, 35 and 39 Engineer

Regiments, 59 and 131(V) Commando Squadrons, 516 STRE (Bulk Petroleum), 521 STRE (Water Development) and 522 STRE (Works) as well as Geographic support. All made an outstanding contribution to the exercise – in temperatures reaching 50°C – constructing the infrastructure and camps for the joint forces. None of this would have been achieved without the logistics support provided by 45 Field Support Squadron, which, having worked in the desert from late May to December without a break, could truly claim to have been 'first in last out'.

A more seminal event was to occur in the latter part of 2001. On 11 September, Muslim terrorists attacked the World Trade Center in New York and the Pentagon in Washington by crashing hijacked airliners into them. This instigated a complete reappraisal in the manner and conduct of war. The apparent outcome was perceived to be a protracted conflict against terrorism in the shadow of a revised cold war of ideologies based on religion. This fundamentally affected the nature of subsequent military operations and caused the structure of the army to be critically examined in the light of this new asymmetric security threat. It was assessed that the attack had been mounted by Al-Qaida personnel trained in Afghanistan. As a consequence, operations were begun against Al-Qaida/Taliban using the convenience of a forward mounting base from Exercise 'Saif Sareea 2'. In March 2002, 59 Independent Commando Squadron and a detachment from 49 Field Squadron (EOD) deployed to Afghanistan on Operation 'Jacana' to provide close and general engineer support to 45 Commando Group, conducting warfighting operations against remaining pockets of Al-Qaida and Taliban fighters. Subsequently HQRE 3rd (UK) Division and

A tented camp of the type constructed by the Corps at such places as Basra and Mazor-e-Sharif.

elements of 36 Engineer Regiment deployed to Afghanistan on Operation 'Fingal' as part of the International Security Assistance Force to Afghanistan to assist in providing a secure environment for the interim administration of the country, thereby allowing political and diplomatic dialogue to continue. Specialist support was provided by 34 Field Squadron (Air Support) as the Lead Air Support Squadron, 49 Field Squadron (EOD) and a large element of the Military Works Force. 36 Engineer Regiment Group was relieved by 26 Engineer Regiment, which in turn handed over to 60 HQ and Support Squadron and 48 Field Squadron (Air Support).

By late 2002 the Corps could see an end to the Strategic Defence Review implementation, the last three squadrons being due to form up during 2003. The Regimental HQ of 23 Engineer Regiment and 12 (Nova Scotia) Headquarters Squadron had already started to form at Waterbeach and were intended to declare Full Operating Capability in August 2003. 10 Field Squadron (Air Support) was forming at RAF Leeming and 30 Field Squadron would form up by December. 522 STRE (Works) had moved to Chilwell, and 517 STRE (Bulk Petroleum) would form in 2003 as planned. Regrettably the formation of 52 Independent Field Squadron (Air Support) was a casualty of achievable manning levels. On the positive side, 33 Engineer Regiment (EOD) received an additional 72 men and women over 2002 and 2003. The RE Trials and Development Unit would also receive manpower increments over the lifetime of the introduction of new tracked engineer equipment.

However, the burgeoning need for manpower confirmed that the rate at which

the Corps would grow 'on paper' over 2003 could not be matched by the increases in throughput of the recruiting and training organizations. In addition, the average tour interval for the Corps had decreased to ten months in 2002. Given that the average tour intervals for the majority of close-support engineer regiments was 24 months, the deficit was more keenly felt by the general support and specialist units. Territorial units continued to fill gaps in both officer and soldier posts for deployment on enduring operations – some 30 were deployed in the Balkans in 2002. More ominously, contingency planning had begun to prepare for possible operations in the Middle East, and preparations for operations in the event of a national Fire Brigade Union strike, Operation 'Fresco', were also in hand.

Elsewhere, in Northern Ireland the pace of life and activity, with 'normalization' works and support to public order, resulted in a need for the Roulement Engineer Squadron to be in the province for both summer and winter tours. In Sierra Leone, support to Operation 'Silkman' finished in 2002, and all UK operational support was withdrawn; the UK-led International Monitoring and Training Team continued, with the Corps providing three clerks of works.

2003 was dominated by the Corps' contribution to Operation 'Telic', the invasion of Iraq, which was undertaken to remove the threat of weapons of mass destruction. The Corps' involvement with this operation was a truly extraordinary achievement and is dealt with more fully elsewhere in this book. Suffice to say that the operation drew on 54 per cent of the deployable Corps, representing over 14 per cent of the land forces deployed. In percentage terms, it was the largest operational deployment of Royal Engineers since the Second World War. In addition to unprecedented levels of activity in 2003, the Corps also grew in size with the reformation of 12 (Nova Scotia) HQ Squadron, 10 Field Squadron (Air Support) and 30 Field Squadron. Finally, the creation of a third CRE (Works) (63) and an increase in the Military Works Force establishment was implemented. This latter was key to reducing the short tour intervals within the force, which were becoming a major retention issue. This was just about the end of the enhancements gained in the Review of 1998, but the Engineer-in-Chief's staff were starting to plan another organization under the label of the Future Army Structure.

In addition to fighting a major war in the Middle East, the relentless pace of change continued. One of the continuing challenges was to generate sufficient trained manpower in the short term. The Corps was still suffering from overstretch and poor retention in certain trades, particularly the fitter and signaller trades, and structural problems in the EOD Regiment and Military Works Force that would have to be addressed. Additionally, there were pressures on the ability to deliver trade training at the rate required without enhancements to the Royal School of Military Engineering. At this point, mention should be made of the Territorial Army, which overall had been reduced to just over 41,000, the Corps losing some 56 per cent of its strength. The intention was to make it more usable in supporting the Regular army, particularly with its specialist manpower. The focus for all Territorial regi-

ments and squadrons in 2003 was support for Operations 'Telic 1 and 2', the largest mobilization of the reserve forces since the Second World War. On Operation 'Telic 1', they provided 14 per cent of the Royal Engineers in theatre. In total, 24 per cent of the territorial manpower was deployed on operations during 2003.

The Corps also had to carry out its enduring operational commitments in 2003. In the Balkans, as part of the reduction of troop levels, 26 Engineer Regiment was not replaced in May 2003 on completion of its Operation 'Oculus' tour in Kosovo. The Sapper commitment was reduced to a reinforced, rear-based RE troop to provide close-support to the Operational Reserve Force, an infantry battlegroup. The close-support squadron commitment to Bosnia continued to provide support, with an EOD troop and an STRE (Works), to the new Multi-National Brigade (North West). In Afghanistan, the UK now provided a Provincial Reconstruction Team at Mazar-e-Sharif to create conditions outside Kabul to allow the Afghan administration to operate with the Military Works Force in providing infrastructure support to the team. 45 Field Support Squadron were the last Sapper sub-unit deployed, returning from Afghanistan early in 2003. The requirement to provide the maintenance section in the Falkland Islands continued, and they remained stretched in coping with the level of equipment held in theatre. The Sovereign Base Areas in Cyprus provided essential support to Operation 'Telic', 62 (Cyprus) Support Squadron and elements of the Military Works Force providing significant support to the forces mounted from the island. In Sierra Leone, the UK-led Training Team continued, with a garrison engineer and three clerks of works serving in Operational Commitments Establishment posts. In February, 10 Field Squadron (Air Support) deployed for a month in support of the Spearhead Lead Element, which was responsible for providing additional security at the time when individuals cited for war crimes were due to be tried. 42 Field Squadron deployed in June 2003 for a six-week mission to the Democratic Republic of Congo in support of the French-led European Mission. The squadron took a French Air Support Engineer Troop under command to assist with tasks based on Bunia Airfield; these included the constant, overnight repair of the airfield pavement and the construction of an aircraft apron.

2004 was again dominated by operations. Operation 'Telic' remained the main commitment, but the Corps was also deployed on operations in Afghanistan, the Balkans, Sierra Leone, Northern Ireland and on the UK mainland. Further changes to the army, but particularly the Corps, were in hand under the banner of Future Army Structure. This is dealt with elsewhere in this history, but it was obvious from the inception that it would result in significant structural changes for the Corps. The Corps' multi-capable utility had been recognized, and at a time when many other parts of the army were facing a reduction in strength the Corps would gain much-needed capability. The Corps was still suffering from undermanning, which was being most acutely felt in field units. This was mainly as a result of the previous expansion rather than recruiting difficulties. For the Territorial Army, deployment on Operation 'Telic' continued with two field troops (from 73 and 75 Engineer Regiments (V)) being provided to 35 Engineer Regiment, and one field troop (from 71 Engineer Regiment (V)) being provided to 22 Engineer Regiment. Operation 'Midway', the making safe of Second World War munitions, was supported throughout 2004 by 101 Engineer Regiment (EOD) (V). The Territorial Army continued to support Operation 'Telic 5', which commenced at the end of 2004, by providing the Operation 'Midway' Troop to 33 Engineer Regiment (EOD), and a number of Military Works Force (V) personnel were embedded in the regular specialist teams.

In the United Kingdom the Corps remained busy. In Great Britain, preparations for Operation 'Fresco', the support to cover fire-service strikes, continued until the armed forces were stood down on 27 August. In addition, 33 Engineer Regiment (EOD) was again involved in a range of tasks including searches for the main political party spring and autumn conferences, MOD Main Building, the Scottish Parliament and Leeds Castle for the Anglo-Irish Talks. The regiment also provided a team to search the harbour at Boscastle following the disastrous flood of 18 August. In Northern Ireland there was a marked decrease in terrorist activity, and the 'marching season' passed off with few incidents. The consequent reduction in support to public-order work enabled the Roulement Engineer Squadron, less its Search Troop, to become increasingly based on the mainland, but ready to move at 24-hours notice.

In Iraq the Corps' commitment to peace enforcement operations continued, with Sappers still delivering a broad range of mili-

Operation 'Herrick'. Concrete batching on Kandahar Airfield, Afghanistan.

and 529 STRE (Air Support) deployed to Kandahar International Airport to establish it as a Harrier Deployed Operating Base.

The situation in Bosnia remained stable, and as part of the continued withdrawal of troops across the Balkans 31 Armoured Engineer Squadron and the EOD detachment withdrew in March; the Improvised Explosive Device Detection team followed in mid-May. The pan-Balkan Specialist Team became just a Property Manager and his deputy supporting the Multi-National Task Force (North West). Limited military engineer tasking continued with 33 Engineer Regiment (EOD) providing advance search support to a number of weapon-search tasks, and elements of both 516 and 517 STRE (Bulk Petroleum) deployed to support base closures and the decommissioning of fuel installations. In Kosovo, the sole standing RE commitment was a clerk of works, who was withdrawn in early November. As with Bosnia, the Corps continued to deploy forward as required to support specific operations. The most significant of these was in March when the Spearhead Lead Element deployed at very short notice in response to an unexpected rapid increase in tension between ethnic groups. The battalion was supported by elements of 51 Field Squadron and 33 Engineer Regiment (EOD) for the operation.

tary engineer support across Multi-National Division (South East), including life-support, force protection and EOD. At the tactical level, the Close Support Engineer Regiment remained fully committed, offering technical and project management advice to the public utilities as well as providing Power Support Teams, which played a pivotal part in facilitating repairs to the power grid. In Afghanistan, the standing commitment remained at three clerks of works. In addition, 42 Field Squadron and elements of a Specialist Team deployed to Mazar-e-Sharif in May to construct a 250-man tented camp and improve the infrastructure for the Provincial Reconstruction Team. In September, elements of 53 Field Squadron (Air Support)

In Cyprus and the Falkland Islands, small RE maintenance teams continued to provide support. The scale and nature of the capability in the Falkland Islands was reviewed in May, which led to a welcome reduction in the team to 11 tradesmen; in order to ensure continuity and expertise, 39 Engineer Regiment took on responsibility for the provision of the core of the team.

42 Engineer Regiment (Geographic), in common with the rest of the Corps, continued to support Operation 'Telic' with a Geographic Troop located in Basra International Airport. Members of the New Zealand army geographic personnel augmented the troop for much of 2004, numerous tasks being completed.

2005 was once again dominated by the situation in Iraq, with the Corps fully committed to security support and nation-building operations. Sappers continued to deliver a broad range of military engineer support across the area, including life-support, force protection, riverine operations, Iraqi national infrastructure development, diving, EOD and search. Elsewhere, there was a reduction in the number and scale of standing commitments and a shift towards directed tasks, specifically in the Balkans and Afghanistan, where the Corps continued to provide combat engineer, EOD and infrastructure support to both the Spearhead Lead Element and Airborne Task Force. 12 (Air Support) Engineer Group provided the Lead Air Support Squadron in support of the RAF. The result was an overall improvement in the tour interval for units to an average of two years between operational tours, but it masked the significant pressures that remained on 170 (Infrastructure Support) Engineer Group and 33 Engineer Regiment (EOD). For the Territorial Army, the tempo of mobilizations decreased in 2005. Up to 40 personnel continued to be deployed in support of operations in Iraq, Afghanistan and the Balkans. The Engineer and Logistic Staff Corps provided operational support to the Royal Signals in the UK and to the Corps in Iraq, as well as a wide range of support to training and policy.

At home the Corps provided EOD support to the G8 Summit at Gleneagles in July 2005. A team from 42 Engineer Regiment (Geographic) also provided mapping and terrain analysis to the police, helping to prepare police units that do not routinely operate outside of their normal areas of operation. This operation also saw the first deployment of 25 Engineer Regiment outside Northern Ireland: the regiment provided a Public Order Troop to protect the perimeter fences of HM Naval Base Faslane and Clyde. In addition, 33 Engineer Regiment (EOD) was once again involved in a range of military aid to the civil authority tasks. These included providing troops to support the Metropolitan Police following the 7 July 2005 Muslim terrorist bombings in London, and searches in support of the York Races, the Trafalgar 2000 celebrations and the G8 Home Affairs Conference. In Northern Ireland the decommissioning announcement by the Provisional Irish Republican Army and the signing of the Joint Declaration for Normalization has increased the focus and pace of reducing the military presence in the province.

As the writing of this book ends in December 2005, the Corps is preparing to support 19 Light Brigade's deployment to Afghanistan on Operation 'Herrick' with an engineer group based on 38 Engineer Regiment. Although there has been some talk of withdrawal from Iraq, the commitment is likely to endure for some time, certainly until the newly elected government is able to exercise some authority in the country. One thing is certain – that it will never be a dull career for a Sapper, whatever his rank and employment.

THE IRAQ WAR

Setting aside the political and social controversy that surrounded, and continues to surround, the deployment of United Kingdom forces to the Middle East in 2003, Operation 'Telic' was the largest intervention operation undertaken by UK Forces since the 1991 Gulf War, deploying some 40,000 military personnel.

At the end of the Gulf War in 1991, the United Nations Security Council imposed strict conditions on Iraq, seeking to remove the threat from Saddam Hussein's regime to his neighbouring states. Successive Security Council resolutions required the destruction, removal or rendering useless of Iraqi weapons of mass destruction, a cessation of its repression of Shi'ite Muslim and Kurdish populations but allowed for the sale of enough Iraqi oil to provide food for its population. Northern and Southern no-fly zones were established to stiffen these resolutions. By 1998, evidence showed that Iraq was illegally smuggling oil, and dire consequences were threatened if it continued to violate agreements. The harassment and blocking of weapons inspectors precipitated a four-day bombing campaign on weapon facilities in December 1998. Following the Muslim terrorist attacks on the mainland of the United States on 11 September 2001, President Bush declared war on those who attacked the United States, making no distinction between terrorists and those states that harboured them.

In September 2002, international pressure for the return of the weapons inspectors was bolstered when the UK government published a dossier that purported to detail the extent of Iraq's illegal holdings of weapons and the potential for a missile to strike UK sovereign bases on Cyprus. Later that month, diplomacy apparently failing, contingency planning had begun in both the Ministry of Defence and the Permanent Joint Headquarters to prepare for possible operations in the Middle East.

> *"The containment of Iraq has not succeeded and there must be genuine preparedness to take action."*
> – Prime Minister Tony Blair, September 2002

By November 2002 the international community, led by the United States, and exasperated by Iraq's continuing intransigence and defiance of international law, adopted United Nations Security Council Resolution No. 1441. This declared Iraq to be in breach of previous resolutions and set out new procedures for the conduct of inspections, with the threat of serious consequences if cooperation were not forthcoming. The inspectors were allowed back at the end of the month, but their subsequent reports declared that Iraq had not cooperated; rather it was engaged in systematic concealment and deceit. In December, the Iraqis produced their own documentation detailing their nuclear, biological and chemical activities and formally stated that they had no weapons of mass destruction. The stand-off between the Iraqis and the United Nations continued with the United States in complete disbelief over the documentation submitted and the statements made by the regime.

As the Iraqi regime had failed to comply with the will of the United Nations since

1991, the UK joined an American-led coalition that was preparing to use force as a last resort to secure compliance. On 24 February 2003, the United Kingdom, the United States and Spain tabled a draft resolution making it clear that Iraq had failed to take the opportunity presented in Resolution 1441, but a consensus could not be achieved in the UN Security Council. Notwithstanding the lack of a mandate on the use of force, the UK and US began the deployment of forces to the Middle East in preparation for possible operations. The UK force deployment, built around 1st (UK) Armoured Division, was announced on 20 January 2003. On 7 March 2003, a second revised draft resolution gave Saddam Hussein an ultimatum to disarm by 17 March or face military action. On the due date, America gave Saddam Hussein a further ultimatum to leave Iraq in 48 hours or face war. On 20 March, all avenues having apparently been exhausted, limited airstrikes began on targets associated with the Iraqi regime.

Operation 'Telic' presented one of the greatest challenges to the Corps for many years. Deploying only 12 months after mounting operations in Afghanistan, and concurrent with Operation 'Fresco', the deployment of a three-brigade manoeuvre division to the Middle

East was an immense undertaking. The initial planning for the generation of a military force commenced in mid-2002. Ultimately, by December 2002, with an amphibious landing-force added to the Joint Force Element Table, the Corps was required to give support to all five components – land, air, maritime, logistic and special forces. Included in the order of battle was the newly formed 23 Engineer Regiment (Air Assault). Also at the end of December a decision was made to stop planning for land operations from Turkey (the 'Northern Entry Option') and to concentrate on entry from the south via Kuwait. On completion of the Royal Engineer force package, some 3,500 Sappers of all ranks were earmarked to deploy – 54 per cent of the deployable Corps.

The Territorial Army also played a major part in the operation. In mid-January 2003, ministerial approval was given for the first tranche of territorial and reserve mobilization, totalling nearly 700 officers and soldiers. Later in January the requirement

Aldershot Bridge over the Shatt-al-Arab, Iraq.

for support for 12th (Air Support) Engineer Brigade was significantly increased to around 300 personnel – thus the reserve forces provided substantial support to the operation. This saw not only the provision of more than 500 individual augmentees to Regular units but also the mobilization of 131 Independent Commando Squadron (V), 507 STRE (Railway) (V), 412 Amphibious Troop (V) and elements of 101 Engineer Regiment (EOD) (V). 100 Field Squadron (Militia) and 508 STRE (Works) (V) were subsequently mobilized, complete, for Operation 'Telic 2'.

The UK National Contingent Commander, Air Marshal B. K. Burridge, CBE, adc, and his staff formed the UK National Contingent HQ, which was built on the UK Joint Force HQ, commanded by Brigadier (later Major General) P. A. Wall, CBE, late RE, located in Qatar. Within the HQ, a Joint Force Engineer Staff, under Colonel N. M. Fairclough, OBE, brought together all engineer staff functions and assumed command of all Engineer Force Troops from 64 Works Group, the Joint Force EOD Group and 14 Geographic Squadron. This was the first time that the Joint Force Engineer concept had been used on an operation. Although the campaign was essentially a land battle, the Joint Force Engineer Branch provided a single focus for engineer advice and support to air, naval, logistic and special forces as the operational need required.

This was also the first time that component warfighting was used in anger.

The Maritime Component has commando engineers to support amphibious operations. These perform both combat engineering (mobility and survivability) and force engineering (for example, fuels engineering and route-development) tasks.

Land Component engineers provide a full range of engineering capabilities and generally, at brigade level, provide close-support and focus on mobility, counter-mobility and survivability tasks. Those at divisional level both enhance brigade support and provide general support such as explosive ordnance disposal, water-source development, fuels engineering, infrastructure development and the repair and maintenance of utility services. Geographic engineers exist at brigade level and higher.

The Air Component engineers are trained and organized to provide specialist support to the Royal Air Force by focusing on airfield maintenance and repair, sustainment tasks such as fuel engineering and accommodation and services such as infrastructure and ammunition protection.

Logistic Component engineers specialize in support of the reception, staging, onward movement and integration of the force into theatre and then enhance the facilities and infrastructure necessary to sustain the force. In addition, specialist engineers logistic units are part of the supply chain to manage the provision of all engineer matériel necessary to support engineer activity.

The Special Forces Component does not have engineer units formally allocated to it; specialist support such as EOD and geographic support are provided for specific missions or tasks.

Planning in HQ 3rd Commando Brigade for what was to become Operation 'Telic' began in September 2002. Initially based on a single RM Commando and an Amphibious Ready Group, changes and enhancements to the plan eventually committed 3rd Commando Brigade minus 45 Commando Royal Marines but with 15 (US) Marine Expeditionary Unit under command for the initial phases. First estimates envisaged a high requirement for early general support engineering and EOD. Accordingly, 70 men from 131 Independent Commando Squadron (V) were mobilized, and two EOD teams from 21 Field Squadron (EOD) augmented 49 Field Squadron (EOD). Elements of 516 STRE (Bulk Petroleum) provided fuels engineering support, both in ship-to-shore and oil-infrastructure capability. This grouping, with 59

Independent Commando Squadron, became known as the Brigade Engineer Group and was commanded by Major J. C. Weedon. The initial operation conducted by 3rd Commando Brigade on 21 March 2003 was an opposed helicopter night assault into the Al Faw peninsula to secure the oil infrastructure intact and provide flank protection to the Mine Countermeasures Force clearing the Khawr Abd Allah waterway to Umm Qasr. As the first ground action of the war, the action had strategic significance. After securing the initial objective, the brigade advanced north and was involved in a series of engagements culminating in the fall of Al Basrah. The group played a full part in supporting all units of the brigade to provide initial mine and booby-trap identification as well as minefield breaches on the Al Faw peninsula, assisting with the seizure of the port of Umm Qsar and the Al Faw oil manifold. At the end of decisive operations the group were in great demand throughout the brigade area to

An ambulance convoy crosses the Hawr Al Hammar Canal in Iraq over a bridge of M3 rigs.

provide help in restoring basic amenities.

12th (Air Support) Engineer Brigade provided military engineering support to the Air Component and was well-versed in the types of tasks that it would face, having supported the RAF for some 12 years in the Middle East and being responsible for the enabling works for Exercise 'Saif Sareea 2' in 2001. Planning for air operations in Iraq started in September 2002. Exercise 'Internal Look', a staff exercise held in Qatar, set the strategic context, anticipated the requirement for air support engineering and set up close links with United States Air Force engineers. One key fallout from this exercise was an agreement by HQ LAND that 12th Brigade and its assets would be placed under operational command of Commander-in-Chief Strike Command. Air Component engineers offered additional RE capability beyond that described above: they built the accommodation at the Tallil Coalition Forward Arming and Refuelling Point, which was developed into a deployed operating base, and enabled Basrah International Airport as an Air Point of Disembarkation. Air Component engineers supported the RAF Deployed Operating Bases across the Joint Operational Area, from Seeb and Thumrait in the south, at Fujairah, Al Udeid, Muharraq, Price Sultan Air Base, Al Jabar and Ali Al Salem to Incirlik and Akrotiri in the north.

The reinforced 102 Logistics Brigade formed the basis of the Logistic Component and contained an embedded Headquarters Royal Engineers. The Sappers were from 36 Engineer Regiment and comprised 50 HQ Squadron, 20 Field Squadron, 69 Gurkha Field Squadron and 70 Gurkha Field Support Squadron. Phase 1 of the campaign was to conduct reception and staging operations to enable the force to build up, consolidate and train in theatre.

Considerable works were also carried out to facilitate entry into the Joint Operations Area. Intelligence collection regarding the Iraqi and Kuwait infrastructure was coordinated by the Engineer and Logistics Staff Corps (V). Advice ranged from mitigation of the effects of inundation from the deliberate release of water from dams and reservoirs, to dealing with the hazards presented by oil and gas fires resulting from the destruction of petrochemical facilities. One major task for the infrastructure staff was the construction of tented camp infrastructure in Kuwait, a contract worth US$24,000,000, and the provision of nearly 21,000 bed spaces in the concentration area and 7,000 elsewhere. This task included four 5,000-person kitchens, 1,000 toilets, 100 shower blocks, 40 kilometres of bunds and ten megawatts of power. Other tasks included the construction of ranges, the design of air-conditioning installations, vehicle off-loading ramps, route maintenance and the construction of a field hospital. Logistic Component units were also concerned with Phase 3, Decisive Operations, and Phase 4, the Post Conflict phase, including humanitarian support by constructing another field hospital and prisoner-of-war cages, and assisting displaced civilians, as well as supporting operations in Umm Qasr. Task groups were also formed to look after the operation and maintenance of the hospitals, the Tallil arming and refuelling point, Umm Qasr port and the prisoner-of-war cages.

The component was based on 1st (UK) Armoured Division. 7 Armoured and 16 Air Assault Brigade were under command at the commencement of operations, with 3rd

Commando Brigade joining them later in the campaign. The Division was, with 1st (US) Marine Division, part of the 1st Marine Expeditionary Force, a Corps-level formation tasked with providing flank security to 5th (US) Corps who were providing the main effort in an army group attack towards Baghdad. The Divisional Engineer Group consisted of 23 Engineer Regiment (Air Assault), 32 Engineer Regiment (with a preponderance of armoured engineer capability) providing close-support to 16th and 7th Brigades respectively. 28 Engineer Regiment, 65 Field Support Squadron and 20 and 69 Gurkha Field Squadrons provided the general support capability. Their mission statement was:

'Attack. To provide close and general engineer support to 1st (UK) Armoured Division to defeat enemy forces, secure key oil infrastructure and control the area of operations in order to enable 1st (US) Marine Expeditionary Force operations to continue north without interference.'

Prior to D-day, the Division had conducted planning on securing the oil infrastructure and had carried out training with Engineer and Logistic Staff Corps, EOD, 516 STRE (Bulk Petroleum) and US Marine Corps personnel. As planning proceeded it became clear that the planners, while considering the question of oil, had not considered elements vital to it such as power stations, the potential for booby-traps, the domestic requirement for fuel and the likelihood that the system would be pressurized and live. It was also apparent that the US Marine Corps had little knowledge of the environment they were about to enter. A training scheme

was therefore set up, which used expatriate oilmen and military expertise from 516 STRE (Bulk Petroleum) and the Engineer and Logistic Staff Corps. The mature plan saw the Joint Force EOD group, supported by 516 STRE (Bulk Petroleum) personnel moving into the oilfields in order to render them safe.

President Bush issued his ultimatum to Saddam Hussein to leave within 48 hours on 17 March 2003. The declared D-day was 19 March, and the land assault commenced with 3rd Commando Brigade's operation on the Al Faw peninsula on 21 March 2003. At the same time, 26 Armoured Engineer Squadron opened routes across the border obstacle-belt, allowing 15 Marine Expeditionary Unit to attack the port of Umm Qasr. Almost simultaneously, 39 Armoured Engineer Squadron opened two routes to support 7 Armoured Brigade's advance towards Az Zubayr and Al Basrah. Farther to the west, 61 Field Support Squadron put in a breach to allow the logistic elements of 1 Marine Expeditionary Force and 16th Air Assault Brigade to move north. Once the UK battle groups were called forward by 1st Marine Division, progress north and east was rapid. 16th Air Assault Brigade took over the responsibility of the Rumaylah oilfields while 7th Armoured Brigade relieved an American combat team west of Al Basrah city. By this time 10 Field Squadron had established a forward arming and refuelling point near the town of Safwan for the Joint Helicopter Force.

By 23 March it appeared that the Iraqi army had simply melted away, but British and American forces were now encountering organized paramilitary fighters conducting asymmetric operations against the coalition. An EOD team from 21 Field Squadron (EOD) was ambushed by these irregulars at Az Zubayr, resulting in the deaths of Staff Sergeant Simon Cullingworth and Sapper Luke Allsopp. By 26 March, Az Zubayr had been secured and the four crossing-points on the Shat Al Basrah river were held. In a similar timeframe, 3rd Commando Brigade were advancing north towards Al Basrah along the Al Faw peninsula supported by Challenger 2 tanks ferried across the Shat Al Basrah by 412 Amphibious Troop (V), part of 23 Amphibious Engineer Squadron. This was the first operation for both 412 Troop and for the M3 rig.

With 3rd and 7th Brigades holding a ring around Al Basrah, 16th Air Assault Brigade exploited north to the Euphrates and probed east to Highway 6, a main route to Baghdad, guided by brigade reconnaissance units accompanied by 12 and 50 HQ Squadrons providing engineer reconnaissance teams. Behind the forward line of troops, 69 Gurkha and 20 Field Squadrons had moved into the divisional area to construct a field hospital and a

The Iraq Medal.

prisoner-of-war camp in Umm Qasr town while 528 STRE (Utilities) set about restoring essential services and facilities in the port. By 2 April, 7th Brigade had gained progressively larger footholds in Al Basrah through armoured raiding, supported by AVREs from 32 Engineer Regiment, and combat engineers providing close-support to assault troops. On 6 April, raids across the Shat Al Basrah encountered little organized resistance All four of 7th Brigade's battlegroups struck at the town from the west and 3rd Brigade from the south in Operation 'Sinbad'. UK forces were firm in Al Basrah, and by 9 April the city was quiet and the regime had fallen, symbolized by the toppling of statues of Saddam in Baghdad. Two days later, in a final move, 16th Air Assault Brigade moved north and west to secure the whole of Maysan province.

The ground war was effectively over. However, as we have seen many times in this history, it was time for the Sappers to get out their toolkits and begin Phase 4 – the stabilization, recovery and transition to post-conflict operations.

ORGANIZATION OF THE CORPS

The chain of command at the highest levels of the Corps is as follows:

The Colonel-in-Chief
Chief Royal Engineer
Colonels Commandant
Engineer-in-Chief (Army)

Since the formation of the standing army in 1660, the colonelcy of a regiment of cavalry or infantry was highly esteemed for its prestige and as a source of income – a colonelcy was also sound investment, and they often changed hands for large sums of money. The colonel was the owner of the regiment, and for some years a regiment was known by the name of its colonel – an example being the Green Howards. This did not apply in the Corps of Engineers because, as with the Artillery, it was in effect a private army of the Board of Ordnance. Engineer officers did not receive military rank until 1757.

However, with the development of the standing army, the status of the colonel began to change with a gradual shift to more central control, away from a regimental basis. Nevertheless, the colonel was still important and powerful, and so evolved the post of colonel-in-chief as a sort of figurehead of a regiment. It became customary that this post be given to a senior officer, sometimes retired, who had achieved high honour and prominence within either the army or affairs of the nation. Although all soldiers swear allegiance to the sovereign at the start of their service in the army, the sovereign (or other royal personages) may honour a regiment or corps by becoming its colonel-in-chief. The first colonel-in-chief of the newly amalgamated Corps of Royal Engineers was His Royal Highness The Duke of Cambridge, from 1861 to 1904. His Majesty King Edward VII then became the first sovereign to assume the post, and this has continued with succeeding sovereigns.

The Chief Military Engineer has had various titles since the earliest days when Bishop Gundulph was titled 'The King's Chief Engineer'. There followed Chief Engineers, Inspector-Generals of Fortifications, Directors of Fortifications and Works, and other similar titles. With the continuing evolution and modernization of the military it was decided in 1936 to re-create the post of Chief Royal Engineer. His Majesty the King selected General Sir Bindon Blood, GCB, GCVO, to fill

this new post. He had been commissioned into the Royal Engineers in 1860 and had a distinguished active career until he retired in 1907 aged 65 – he was thus 94 years old when appointed Chief Royal Engineer! He resigned in 1940 and died a month later, aged 97. The Chief Royal Engineer is a distinguished officer of the Corps and Head of the Corps of Royal Engineers, and his tenure is normally for a period of five years. He is responsible for seeing that the traditions and customs are preserved and provides the continuity to important matters of Corps policy; he also maintains contact with other Corps of Engineers in the Commonwealth and ensures that the colonel-in-chief is briefed on Corps matters. He will usually have previously served as a colonel commandant.

In the early 19th century the strength of the Corps was reckoned in battalions, and colonels commandant were appointed to command them. These posts were much sought-after by generals and other senior officers for the high rate of pay that they attracted. After 1874, the battalion system of reckoning strength was changed, and in 1881 the special pay for colonels commandant was dispensed with. Since then the appointment has been honorary, a valued method of honouring a distinguished officer's service. The current establishment is for twelve colonels commandant, one of whom, with the colonel-in-chief's approval, is appointed Representative Colonel Commandant for a year. He thus assists the Chief Royal Engineer in the proper representation of the Corps at official ceremonies and functions. The upper age limit for colonels commandant is 65.

With military and technical affairs becoming more complicated it was necessary to improve engineer representation at the higher command level of the army. Thus the post of Engineer-in-Chief was established in 1941 and was held by a major general until 1995 when it was reduced to brigadier. As an Arms Director, he is the professional head of the Corps, acting as engineer adviser to the Chief of the General Staff, and to the Royal Navy and Royal Air Force on matters of military engineering on behalf of the Chief of the General Staff.

Throughout this history of the Corps, mention has been made of Commonwealth Engineer activities. The Corps has formal affiliations with:

The Canadian Military Engineers
The Corps of Royal Australian Engineers
The Corps of Royal New Zealand
 Engineers
Indian Engineers
Pakistan Engineers
The Sri Lanka Engineers
Malaysian Engineer Corps
Zambia Corps of Engineers
The Corps of Fiji Engineers
The Queen's Gurkha Engineers

When the Depot of the Royal Sappers and Miners moved from Woolwich to Chatham in 1856 the Depot Brass Band, which had been in existence since 1836, came with them. At Chatham it quickly grew into a military band, and some of the musicians also formed a string orchestra. Its very high reputation continues to this day. Various semi-official volunteer bands have existed from time to time in various stations, but in 1949 a second band was authorized and it became the RE Band (Aldershot), the original band becoming the RE Band (Chatham). Reductions in establishments saw the two bands

amalgamated in 1985 and again based at Chatham. In 1994, as part of a review of military music, the band's establishment was reduced from 49 to 35. It has a very heavy programme of visits to Royal Engineer units and other armies worldwide, and it takes its place alongside the combatant side of the Corps on operations, members having roles as regimental medics and stretcher-bearers. It was mobilized in 2003 for Operation 'Telic' and deployed to Iraq with 16 Air Assault Medical Regiment. The band is the only part of the Corps to wear full ceremonial dress. 71 Engineer Regiment (V), the Scottish TA regiment, has an un-established pipe band, and under the Future Army Structure changes a second band was authorized. This will be a Territorial Army band and will be based in Nottingham with 73 Engineer Regiment (Volunteers).

The Territorial Army is descended from the old Volunteers and Militia raised for home service in emergencies. During the Boer War of 1899–1902 it provided units for active service in South Africa. In 1908 the Territorial Force came into being as part of the far-reaching Haldane army reforms of 1904. These made the old volunteer units a reserve for the Regular army and liable for overseas service, and created a Reserve Army organized in much the same way as the Regulars but with a primary role of home defence. The first test came with the outbreak of the Great War in 1914, when the reserves and Territorial Force were mobilized for overseas service. They served with distinction throughout the war. The Territorials were reorganized and re-equipped to the same standard as the Regulars in the 1930s. They were mobilized in 1939 on the outbreak of the Second

The RE Band.

World War and again served with distinction throughout the conflict. The Territorial Army continues as a reserve force to the Regular army to this day, and many Corps reserve units have distinguished histories in their own rights.

During the Cold War, territorial units fell into two main categories. The Independent Units were self-contained and organized on a local basis, each having its own centre and Regular army permanent staff. Training was spread over evenings and weekends plus a two-week summer camp, up to a set number of training days. The second category comprised the Specialist Units, which were recruited country-wide. They consisted of trained specialists whose function was to use their professional civilian expertise for military purposes. Civil, mechanical and electrical engineers, geologists and members of the oil industry were typical. They undertook military training annually as arranged by the Central Volunteer Headquarters. The main role of both categories was to provide formed units to reinforce Regular army formations.

Under the 1991 Options for Change, there were unit enhancements, particularly in the Airfield Damage Repair role, but two Brigade HQs were lost. Under the 1998 Strategic Defence Review, the considerable Regular army enhancements were at the expense of the Territorial Army, whose manpower was reduced by 56 per cent.

FREEDOMS GRANTED TO THE CORPS OF ROYAL ENGINEERS

	Civic Authority	Type	Date	Present Unit/Holder	Original Unit/Holder
1	Airdrie Borough	Unit	1975	124 Fd Sqn (V)	
2	Aldershot Borough	Corps	1965	RSME (Minley)	11 Engr Gp
3	Barnet Borough	Corps	1982	PCD RLC	PCD RE
4	Beckenham Borough	Unit	1950	211 Fd Sqn (V)	
5	Bethnal Green	Unit	1961	217 Fd Sqn (V)	114 Engr Regt (AER)
6	Birkenhead	Unit	1960	107 Fd Sqn (V)	113 Army Engr Regt (V)
7	Bradford	Unit	1969		
8	Chatham Borough	Corps	1962	RE HQ Mess	
9	Chelsea	Unit	1960	101 Engr Regt (EOD) (V)	101 Fd Engr Regt (TA)
10	Christchurch	Unit	1969	MEXE Christchurch	
11	Edinburgh City		1968		
12	Epsom and Ewell	Unit	1999	135 Indep Geo Sqn (V)	
13	Gibraltar	Corps	1972	1st Fortress STRE	
14	Gillingham Borough	Corps	1953	RE HQ Mess	
15	Hameln Stadt	Corps	1977	28 Engr Regt	28 Engr Regt
16	Harrow Borough	Unit	1983	131 Indep Cdo Sqn RE(V)	
17	Iserlohn Stadt	Corps	1987	RE HQ Mess	26 Engr Regt
18	Jersey (Privilege)	Unit	1995	Jersey Fd Sqn (M)	
19	Kentville Town (NS)	Unit	1990	69 Gurkha Fd Sqn	69 Gurkha Fd Sqn
20	Lewes	Unit		127 Fd Sqn (V)	
21	Lion-Sur-Mer-Ville	Corps	1989	32 Engr Regt	32 Armd Engr Regt
22	Maidstone Borough	Corps	1965	36 Engr Regt	
23	Medway Borough	Corps	1977	HQ RSME	
24	Monmouth	Unit	1953	R Mon RE (M)	
25	Newbury	Corps	1999	42 Svy Engr Gp	
26	Nienburg Stadt	Corps	1980	21 Engr Regt	
27	Oldham	Unit	1999	75 Engr Regt(V)	
28	Osnabrück Stadt	Corps	1957	21 Engr Regt	38 Corps Engr Regt
29	Paderborn Stadt	Corps	1964	35 Engr Regt	4 Div Engrs
30	Ripon City	Corps	1949	38 Engr Regt	
31	Rochester City	Corps	1954	RE HQ Mess	
32	Rochester City	Unit	1961	221 Fd Sqn (EOD) (V)	590 EOD Sqn (V)
33	Rochester City Adoption	Unit	1971	590 STRE (EOD) (V)	
34	Rochester Upon Medway	Unit	1986	69 Gurkha Fd Sqn	
35	Rowley Regis Borough	Unit	1955	215 Coy	215 Plant Sqn (TA)
36	Rushmoor Borough	Corps	1981	RSME (Minley)	11 Engr Gp
37	Sandwich	Corps	2004	1 RSME Regt	1 RSME Regt
38	Seaford	Unit	1959	210 Fd Sqn (TA)	210 Fd Sqn (TA)
39	Sherwood Borough	Unit		575 Fd Sqn RE (V)	
40	Spandaü	Unit	1988	38 (Berlin) Field Squadron RE	
41	Stratford-upon-Avon	Unit	1959	HQ Engineer Resources	
42	Test Valley		1982	22 Engineer Regiment	
43	Weymouth and Portland		1984	RHQ RE	

Under local government reorganizations in 1974, some towns and boroughs amalgamated, so that Freedoms were re-granted in the name of the new authority: for example, Rochester, Chatham and Strood became Medway, and Aldershot joined with Farnborough to become Rushmoor. In addition, many TA units have been honoured in their own right by their home towns.

Enabling and logistic specialist engineers were retained in the shape of seven Specialist Teams RE, two regiments allocated to air support and one retained for EOD. From 1991, their roles started to change, individuals and sub-units being used to reinforce Regular units on operations. The changes for the army, announced in 2004 under the Future Army Structure,

Freedom of Barnet Parade, 1993.

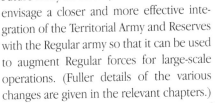

envisage a closer and more effective integration of the Territorial Army and Reserves with the Regular army so that it can be used to augment Regular forces for large-scale operations. (Fuller details of the various changes are given in the relevant chapters.)

One Territorial unit reversed a piece of Corps history. Technology made the antiaircraft searchlight obsolete, but towards the end of the Second World War a system of using searchlights to diffuse light at low elevations was developed to illuminate the battlefield at night. This 'artificial moonlight' was called Movement Light because it assisted movement at night. It was decided that the Royal Engineers should operate this system, and in 1961 a searchlight unit was formed, 873 Movement Light Squadron RE(V). The squadron was disbanded in 1993, and the capability was relocated to the Royal Monmouthshire Royal Engineers (Militia) and 71 Engineer Regiment(V). Under current plans, the capability will not be replaced when the searchlights reach the end of their lives.

From the very earliest times, the City of London has enjoyed various rights and privileges, one of which was to close the city's gates against the sovereign's troops. To this day, whenever bodies of armed troops, or indeed Her Majesty herself, wish to pass over the city's boundaries, the prior permission of the Lord Mayor has to be obtained. However, certain regiments, who have close connections with the city, have been granted the privilege of marching with ceremony through the city. This practice has been copied by other cities, towns and boroughs (but they do not have the right to restrict the Queen's troops as does the City of London). Over the years it has become the practice for a town or corporation to grant what has become known as the Freedom of that town to a military unit to march through the streets on ceremonial occasions with 'drums beating, Colours flying and bayonets fixed'. As a Corps, we do not carry Colours, so our Freedoms are exercised 'with drums beating and bayonets fixed'. This is a particularly gracious way of honouring a regiment and marking its close association with a particular locality – so much so that the practice has been copied abroad, notably in Germany, where British troops have been stationed for so long. The granting of a Freedom is usually carried out with great ceremony, appropriate mementoes of the occasion being exchanged. For the military units this is usually a silver casket containing the parchment Freedom scroll. Freedoms granted to the Corps and the units entrusted are shown opposite.

Under Local Government reorganizations in 1974, some towns and boroughs amalgamated so that Freedoms were re-granted in the name of the new authority; for example Rochester, Chatham and Strood became Medway, while Aldershot joined with Farnborough to become Rushmoor. In addition, many TA units have been honoured in their own right by their home towns.

ESPRIT DE CORPS

In 1906 a number of serving and retired warrant officers and senior non-commissioned officers formed themselves into an association for the purpose of holding an annual reunion dinner in London for all ranks. These reunions were so successful that in 1912 it was decided to form the Royal Engineers Old Comrades Association for all retired members of the Corps. The aims of the Association were, and are, to promote the efficiency of the Corps, foster *esprit de corps* and comradeship, and to render practical or financial assistance to former members of the Corps and their dependants who fall on hard times. This is

The Ravelin Building.

borne out by the motto of the Association:

Service – Not Self

In 1952 the title was changed to Royal Engineers Association. Branches of the Association are to be found throughout the UK and overseas, and its badge is modelled on the Corps cap badge.

The Corps' Library and Archive is co-located with the RE Museum adjacent to Brompton Barracks. It is both a reference and lending library and holds a wealth of material on the Corps and other general military topics.

The RE Museum was first approved in 1875, but at first it lacked proper accommodation. In 1908 the Model Room (now part of Command Wing) in Brompton Barracks, Chatham, was converted into a proper

REA Standards at the Crimea Arch, Brompton.

museum and added to over the years. The main hall had originally been the chapel of the barracks, built in 1806. At the end of the 1980s, the Ravelin Building (previously the Electrical School) adjacent to Brompton Barracks became available, allowing the museum to move into larger premises. Large items of equipment are now displayed, and the collection covers the multitude of activities carried out by the Corps and its predecessors from the Norman conquest to the present day.

The official *History of the Corps of Royal Engineers* currently consists of 11 volumes up to 1980. Volume 12, due for publication in early 2007, will cover the story of the Corps from 1980 to 2000. It is set against the background of Britain's consolidation of her commitment to NATO under the threat of nuclear war, the new concept of strategic mobility in Germany and the equipment that the Corps received. It also covers the increasing commitment to support the Royal Air Force, the collapse of the Warsaw Pact, the series of defence reviews that occurred over the period, as well as the expeditionary operations to the Falkland Islands and the Gulf. The Northern Ireland

campaign is examined up to the cessation of violence, as are the extended Balkans operations. Survey, the reserves and the continuing colonial heritage also have chapters.

The Sapper, the regimental magazine of the Corps, was started in 1895 by three corporals – Piggott, Avis and Beaumont. The War Office subsequently gave approval to its publication as a monthly magazine for the rank and file of the Corps, and it was one of the first of its kind in the army. The first edition, printed at the School of Military Engineering Printing School on 1 August 1895, was of 3,000 copies, all of which sold within a week. The Sapper is now the regimental journal of the Corps and the official organ of the Royal Engineers Association, published bi-monthly.

The Royal Engineers Journal is published three times a year and contains technical and historical articles of Corps interest. Its supplement, published bi-monthly, is a Gazette to keep members of the Institution of Royal Engineers up to date with all manner of items of interest, such as honours and awards, births, deaths and marriages, notices of meetings, dinners, etc., and for a small fee members may also use it for advertising.

Above: The Sapper; *centre,* The Royal Engineers Journal; *top,* The Supplement to the Royal Engineers Journal.

NEW BEGINNINGS: AN ARMY FOR THE FUTURE

In July 2004, the Chief of the General Staff announced the development of a new structure for the army, to be called the Future Army Structure; a proposal to rebalance the army to make it better able to meet the threats of the 21st century. It was to do this by ensuring that the army was equipped with a range of deployable, agile and flexible heavy, medium and light forces, trained and organized to meet the demands of expeditionary operations across the full spectrum of military tasks.

"The new structure will deliver an Army fit for the challenges of the 21st century."
– Secretary of State for Defence, July 2004

There were to be reductions in heavy armour, artillery and infantry, with increases in those key specialists without which the army could not deploy and sustain itself.

There were a number of fundamental changes. The first was a move away from inherited Cold War structures towards a balanced force organized around two armoured brigades, three mechanized brigades, a light and an air-assault brigade. The second element of the reorganization was to make the army more robust and resilient, better able to sustain the enduring expeditionary operations that were now commonplace. This required an enhancement in other key combat and combat service support capabilities, including engineers.

This was a hugely ambitious programme. Much of the manpower for the new structure was to come from Northern Ireland normalization, the release of units that were no longer required to support the police. Examination of almost every army establishment allowed the redistribution of some 10,000 posts, and the routine movement and change of role of infantry battalions was abandoned. Finally, there was to be an impressive re-equipment programme. This would introduce new communications equipment, intelligence collection, electronic-warfare capability, modern reconnaissance and liaison vehicles and a new armoured fighting vehicle programme, called the Future Rapid Effect System.

The Corps benefited extremely well from the proposals, with some far-reaching changes. The Corps' manpower establishment is set to increase by 76 officers and nearly 500 other ranks, and, together with Northern Ireland normalization, an extra 900 all ranks will be delivered to the Corps' field army capability.

The main changes to the Corps' close support units are as follows.

38 Engineer Regiment becomes light role, less 11 Field Squadron, which will remain mechanized in the short term.

23 Engineer Regiment (Air Assault) will finally form officially at Rock Barracks, Woodbridge, with its already-designated component units, plus the new 51 Parachute Squadron.

The creation of 24 Commando Engineer Regiment is spread across the whole new structure implementation period. In the short term, 59 Independent Commando Squadron will gain an extra troop, a small implementation team will be formed, and the whole new organization should be in place by 2010.

The medium and heavy close-support regiments will move to a common structure of three armoured squadrons, each with one armoured, one field and one support troop. To achieve this, 27 and 52 Armoured Engineer Squadrons will be formed and added to 22 and 26 Engineer Regiments.

The reconnaissance troops of General Support Regiments will be disestablished and the capability transferred to Royal Armoured Corps formation reconnaissance regiments.

Field Support Squadrons will gain complete Resources Troops, thus acknowledging the worth of the Resources Specialist trade on expeditionary operations.

33 Engineer Regiment (EOD) will have an extra squadron, 17 Field Squadron (EOD).

On completion of normalization, 25 Engineer Regiment will re-role to provide the second Air Support regiment, which will include 43 Headquarters and Support Squadron, but 33 Field Squadron will be disbanded.

170 (Infrastructure Support) Engineer Group will have a small increase of fifteen posts and will also gain 535 Specialist Team RE (Works) on completion of Northern Ireland normalization. A Force Protection Engineering Cell will also be added.

42 Engineer Regiment (Geographic) will gain 62 posts.

The RE Territorial Army will be more closely integrated with the regular units of the Corps, with stronger affiliations than at present. Its role will change to augmentation of regular units deploying on large-scale operations and the provision of formed sub-units for discrete tasks. The posts requiring augmentation are those that lend endurance and robustness to unit establishments, and these reflect the skills that can most readily be provided by the Territorials.

Their strength is to increase by 47 per cent, and the future organization will comprise The Royal Monmouthshire Royal Engineers (Militia), 71 Engineer Regiment (Air Support) (V), 72 Engineer Regiment (V), 73 Engineer Regiment (Air Support) (V), 75 Engineer Regiment (V), 101 Engineer Regiment (EOD) (V), 131 Independent Commando Squadron RE (V), 135 Independent Geographic Squadron RE (V),

65 Works Group (V), 412 Amphibious Engineer Troop (V), 591 Independent Field Squadron (V) with additional personnel in HQ 170 (Infrastructure Support) Engineer Group and 62, 63 and 64 Works Groups. In addition there will be a troop in Orkney formed from an existing infantry Assault Pioneer Platoon, and, as previously mentioned, the Corps is also to gain a TA Band, which will be co-located with RHQ 73 Engineer Regiment (Volunteers) in Nottingham. Lastly, a TA Parachute Engineer Squadron has been formed in Wakefield.

In addition, 8th Force Engineer Brigade, which historically can trace its origins back to the Engineers that supported the Eighth Army through the Western Desert, via Sicily and thence into Italy, was formed from the former HQ RE Theatre Troops, with some of its policy functions being subsumed into HQ Engineer-in-Chief (Army). The new Brigade HQ has three specific roles. First, it is a peacetime independent headquarters commanding all the LAND Command specialist engineers within three different Engineer Groups and with coordinating authority over 1st and 3rd Division Engineer Groups. The three groups are 12th (Air Support) Engineer Group, 29th (Land Support) Engineer Group and 170th (Infrastructure Support) Engineer Group. Second, it provides the standing Joint Force Engineer and his staff for any deployment of the Permanent Joint Headquarters. Finally, it is a deployable headquarters capable of commanding any forces, not necessarily engineers, assigned to it on operations.

ANNEX I.
THE VICTORIA CROSSES OF THE CORPS

There is a saying, 'Once a Sapper, always a Sapper', meaning military engineers, whatever their rank, speciality or national allegiance. As a Corps, we thus celebrate all 55 Victoria Crosses won by Royal Engineers, Royal Sappers and Miners, members of the Empire and Commonwealth Engineer Corps – and others who won their awards while wearing other cap badges.

Sapper Adam Archibald (Royal Engineers)
Born 14 January 1879; died 11 March 1957. Won VC on the Sambre–Oise Canal, 4 November 1918.

Captain Fenton John Aylmer (Royal (Bengal) Engineers)
Born 5 April 1862; died 3 September 1935. Won VC at Hunza-Nagar on 2 December 1891.

Corporal Cyril Royston Guyton Bassett
(New Zealand Engineers)
Born 3 January 1892; died 9 January 1983. Won VC at Gallipoli, on 7 August 1915.

Lieutenant Mark Sever Bell (Royal Engineers)
Born 15 May 1843; died 26 June 1906. Won VC at Ordahsu, Gold Coast on 4 February 1874.

Second Lieutenant Premindra Singh Bhagat
(Royal Bombay Sappers and Miners)
Born 14 October 1918; died 23 May 1975. Won VC near Metemma, Abyssinia, 31 January to 1 February 1941.

Sergeant John Carmichael (North Staffordshire Regiment)[1]
Born 1 April 1893; died 26 December 1977. Won VC at Hill 60, Belgium, on 8 September 1917.

Lieutenant John Rouse Merriott Chard (Royal Engineers)
Born 21 December 1847; died 1 November 1897. Won VC at Rorke's Drift, Natal, on 22/3 January 1879.

Major Brett Mackay Cloutman (Royal Engineers)
Born 7 November 1891; died 15 August 1971. Won VC at Quartes Bridge at Pont-sur-Sambre on 6 November 1918.

Brigadier-General Clifford Coffin (Royal Engineers)
Born 10 February 1870; died 4 February 1959. Won VC at Westhoek Ridge, Ypres, on 31 July 1917.

Lieutenant James Morris Colquhoun Colvin
(Royal (Bengal) Engineers)
Born 26 August 1870; died 7 December 1945. Won VC at Bilot, Mamund Valley, India (now Pakistan), on 16 September 1897.

Corporal James Lennox Dawson (Royal Engineers)
Born 25 December 1891; died 15 February 1967. Won VC at Loos on 13 October 1915.

Lieutenant Robert James Thomas Digby Jones
(Royal Engineers)
Born 27 September 1876; died 6 January 1900. Won VC at Wagon Hill, Ladysmith, South Africa, on 6 January 1900.

Lieutenant James Dundas (Royal (Bengal) Engineers)
Born 10 September 1842; died 23 December 1879. Won VC at Dewangiri, Bhutan, on 30 April 1865.

Sergeant Thomas Frank Durrant (Royal Engineers)

Born 17 October 1918; died 28 March 1942. Won VC off St. Nazaire, France, on 27/8 March 1942.

Lieutenant Howard Crawfurd Elphinstone
(Royal Engineers)
Born 12 December 1829; died 8 March 1890. Won VC at Sebastopol, Crimea, on 18 June 1855.

Major George de Cardonnel Elmsall Findlay
(Royal Engineers)
Born 20 August 1889; died 26 June 1967. Won VC on the Sambre-Oise Canal, on 4 November 1918.

Sergeant Samuel Forsyth (New Zealand Engineers)
Born 3 April 1891; died 24 August 1918. Won VC at Grevillers, France, on 24 August 1918.

Lieutenant Charles Augustus Goodfellow
(Royal (Bombay) Engineers)
Born 27 November 1836; died 1 September 1915. Won VC at Kathiawar, India, on 6 October 1859.

Lieutenant Gerald Graham (Royal Engineers)
Born 27 June 1831; died 17 December 1899. Won VC at Sebastopol, Crimea, on 18 June 1855.

Sapper William Hackett (Royal Engineers)
Born 11 June 1873; died 27 June 1916. Won VC at Givenchy, France, on 22 June 1916. Unit: 254 Tunnelling Company.

Lieutenant Reginald Clare Hart (Royal (Bengal) Engineers)
Born 11 June 1848; died 19 October 1931. Won VC in the Bazar Valley, Afghanistan, on 31 January 1879.

Private Norman Harvey (Royal Inniskilling Fusiliers)[2]
Born 6 April 1899; died 16 February 1942. Won VC at Ingoyghem, Belgium, on 25 October 1918.

Captain Lanoe George Hawker (Royal Flying Corps)
Born 30 December 1890; died 23 November 1916. Won VC on 25 July 1915.

Lieutenant Duncan Charles Home (Bengal Engineers)
Born 10 June 1828; died 1 October 1857. Won VC at Delhi on 14 September 1857.

Lieutenant James John McLeod Innes (Bengal Engineers)
Born 5 February 1830; died 13 December 1907. Won VC at Sultanpore, India, on 23 February 1858.

Lance-Corporal Charles Alfred Jarvis (Royal Engineers)
Born 29 March 1881; died 19 November 1948. Won VC at Jemappes, Belgium, on 23 August 1914.

Second Lieutenant Frederick Henry Johnson
(Royal Engineers)
Born 15 August 1890; died 26 November 1917. Won VC at Loos on 25 September 1915.

129

Captain William Henry Johnston (Royal Engineers) Born 21 December 1879; died 8 June 1915. Won VC at Missy, near Moulin des Roches, River Aisne, France, on 14 September 1914.

Corporal Frank Howard Kirby (Royal Engineers) Born 12 November 1871; died 8 July 1956. Won VC near Bronkhorstspruit, Delagoa Bay Railway, Pretoria, South Africa, on 2 June 1900.

Second Lieutenant Cecil Leonard Knox (Royal Engineers) Born 9 May 1888; died 4 February 1941. Won VC at Tugny, France, on 22 March 1918.

Captain Edward Pemberton Leach (Royal (Bengal) Engineers) Born 2 April 1847; died 27 January 1913. Won VC at Maidanak, Afghanistan, on 17 March 1879.

Colour Sergeant Peter Leitch (Royal Sappers and Miners) Born August 1820; died 6 December 1892. Won VC at Sebastopol, Crimea, on 18 June 1855.

Corporal William James Lendrim (or Lendrum) (Royal Sappers and Miners) Born 1 January 1830; died 28 November 1891. Won VC at Sebastopol, Crimea, on 14 February 1855.

Lieutenant Wilbraham Oates Lennox (Royal Engineers) Born 4 May 1830; died 7 February 1897. Won VC at Sebastopol, Crimea, on 20 November 1855.

Major Edward Mannock (Royal Air Force)[3] Born 24 May 1887; died 26 July 1918. Won VC in France and Flanders on 17 June 1918.

Second Lieutenant Cyril Gordon Martin (Royal Engineers) Born 19 December 1891; died 14 August 1980. Won VC at Spanbroekmolen, Belgium, on 12 March 1915.

Captain James Thomas Byford McCudden (Royal Flying Corps)[4] Born 28 March 1895; died 9 July 1918. Won VC in northern France on 2 April 1918.

Colour Sergeant Henry McDonald (Royal Sappers and Miners) Born 28 May 1823; died 15 February 1893. Won VC at Sebastopol on 19 April 1855.

Corporal James McPhie (Royal Engineers) Born 18 December 1894; died 14 October 1918. Won VC on the Canal de la Sensée on 14 October 1918.

Captain Coulson Norman Mitchell (Royal Canadian Engineers) Born 11 December 1889; died 17 November 1978. Won VC on the Canal de l'Escaut, north-east of Cambrai, on 8–9 October 1918.

Lieutenant Philip Neame (Royal Engineers) Born 12 December 1888; died 28 April 1978. Won VC at Neuve-Chapelle, France, on 19 December 1914.

Lieutenant-Colonel Augustus Charles Newman (The Essex Regiment)[5] Born 19 August 1904; died 26 April 1972. Won VC at St Nazaire, France, on 27–28 March 1942.

Private John Perie (Royal Sappers and Miners) Born August 1829; died 17 September 1874. Won VC at Sebastopol on 18 June 1855.

Lieutenant Harry North Dalrymple Prendergast (Madras Engineers) Born 15 October 1834; died 24 July 1913. Won VC at Mundisore, India, on 21 November 1857.

Lieutenant Claud Raymond (Royal Engineers) Born 2 October 1923; died 22 March 1945. Won VC at Talaku, Burma, on 22 March 1945.

Corporal John Ross (Royal Sappers and Miners) Born 1822; died 23 October 1879. Won VC at Sebastopol on 21 July 1855.

Lieutenant Philip Salkeld (Bengal Engineers) Born 13 October 1830; died 10 October 1857. Won VC at Delhi on 14 September 1857.

Corporal Michael Sleavon (Royal Engineers) Born 1827; died 14 August 1902. Won VC at Jhansi, India, on 3 April 1858.

Sergeant John Smith (Bengal Sappers and Miners) Born February 1814; died 26 June 1864. Won VC at Delhi on morning of 14 September 1857, preparatory to the assault.

Second Lieutenant Edward Talbot Thackeray (Bengal Engineers) Born 19 October 1836; died 3 September 1927. Won VC at Delhi on 16 September 1857.

Captain Alfred Maurice Toye (The Middlesex Regiment)[6] Born 15 April 1897; died 6 September 1955. Won VC at Eterpigny Ridge, France, on 25 March 1918.

Captain William Spottiswoode Trevor (Royal (Bengal) Engineers) Born 9 October 1831; died 2 November 1907. Won VC at Dewangiri, Bhutan, on 30 April 1865.

Major Arnold Horace Santo Waters (Royal Engineers) Born 23 September 1886; died 22 January 1981. Won VC on the Sambre-Oise canal near Ors, France, on 4 November 1918.

Lieutenant Thomas Colclough Watson (Royal (Bengal) Engineers) Born 11 April 1867; died 15 June 1917. Won VC at Bilot, Mamund Valley, India, on 16 September 1897.

Captain Theodore Wright (Royal Engineers) Born 15 May 1883; died 14 September 1914. Won VC at Mons on 23 August 1914 and Vailly on 14 September 1914.

1   Originally enlisted into the Royal Engineers.
2   Transferred into the Royal Engineers later in his career.
3   Originally a sergeant in the RAMC(TA); commissioned into the Corps in June 1916.
4   Boy Bugler in the Corps 1910–13.
5   Post-war member of the Engineer and Railway Staff Corps.
6   Boy Trumpeter in the Corps 1911–15.

ANNEX 2.
THE GEORGE CROSSES OF THE CORPS

The George Cross was instituted by HM King George VI on 24 September 1940, and, although not intended as such, is widely regarded as the 'civilian VC', being for acts of gallantry not in the face of the enemy. The first six received by members of the Corps were medals given in exchange for the Empire Gallantry Medals they had previously been awarded. Had they been alive, members of the Corps who held either the Albert Medal or the Edward Medal would also have had their medals exchanged

Empire Gallantry Medals exchanged for the George Cross

Major H. E. Burton, OBE
30 June 1924
Lieutenant Colonel J. Stewart, OBE
26 June 1928

Lieutenant E. W. Reynolds
17 September 1940
Second Lieutenant W. L. Andrews
17 September 1940

Second Lieutenant E. E. A. Talbot
17 September 1940
Sergeant W. Burton
17 September 1940

The George Cross

Lieutenant R. Davies
30 September 1940
Sapper G. C. Wylie
30 September 1940
Lieutenant Colonel A. D. Merriman
3 December 1940
Lieutenant J. M. Patton, RCE
13 December 1940
Lieutenant Colonel R. T. Harris
17 December 1940

Lieutenant H. J. L. Barefoot
22 January 1941
Second Lieutenant A. F. Campbell
22 January 1941
Sergeant M. Gibson
22 January 1941
Captain M. F. Blaney
15 March 1941
Lieutenant B. S. T. Archer
30 September 1941

Captain C. A. J. Martin
11 March 1943
Corporal C. Hendry, RCE
2 April 1943
Subedar Subramaniam, IDSM, QVO, S&M
24 February 1944
Second Lieutenant M. P. Benner
17 June 1958

ANNEX 3. THE CORPS MARCH

Wings

The exact origin of *Wings* as the Corps Regimental March is obscure, but in 1870 the Commandant, School of Military Engineering, unaware that the Corps had been allocated *The British Grenadiers* by the War Office, directed that the Band Committee should adopt a popular air of the day as the Regimental Quick March. The Committee adopted *Wings*. It is a combination of two tunes, scored by Bandmaster Newstead of the Royal Engineers Band, one being from the air *The Path Across the Hills*, a tune of unknown German origin, and the other *Wings*, a contemporary popular song by Miss Dickson. It was not until 1902 that *Wings* was also officially recognized.

ANNEX 4. THE CORPS SONG

Hurrah for the CRE!

The Corps Song originated among Sapper units during the South African War. The words, partly in English and partly in Zulu, are sung to the tune of the traditional South African song *Daer de die ding*. The Zulu words are a complaint that there is too much work for too low wages and little food, and they are leaving.

Good Morning Mr Stevens and Windy
* Notchy Knight*
Hurrah for the CRE
We're working very hard, down at
* Upnor Hard*
Hurrah for the CRE
You make fast, I make fast, make fast
* the dinghy*

Make fast the dinghy, make fast the
* dinghy*
You make fast, I make fast, make fast
* the dinghy*
Make fast the dinghy pontoon
For we're marching on to Laffan's Plain
To Laffan's Plain, to Laffan's Plain
Where they don't know mud from clay
Ah, Ah, Ah, Ah, Ah, Ah, Ah, Ah,
Ooshta, ooshta, ooshta, ooshta
Ikona malee, picaninny skoff
Ma-ninga sabenza, here's another off
Oolum-da cried Matabele
Oolum-da, away we go
Ah, Ah, Ah, Ah, Ah, Ah, Ah
Shuush .... Hooray!